FIGHT
FAITHFULLY

The Strength It Takes to Keep Fighting
When No One Can See Your Pain

A memoir by

MELISSA MARKS

WESTBOW
PRESS®
A DIVISION OF THOMAS NELSON
& ZONDERVAN

This book is a work of non-fiction. Unless otherwise noted, the author and the publisher make no explicit guarantees as to the accuracy of the information contained in this book and in some cases, names of people and places have been altered to protect their privacy.

WestBow Press books may be ordered through booksellers or by contacting:

WestBow Press
A Division of Thomas Nelson & Zondervan
1663 Liberty Drive
Bloomington, IN 47403
www.westbowpress.com
844-714-3454

ISBN: 978-1-6642-4332-3 (sc)
ISBN: 978-1-6642-4333-0 (hc)
ISBN: 978-1-6642-4331-6 (e)

Library of Congress Control Number: 2021917207

Print information available on the last page.

WestBow Press rev. date: 08/31/2021

I dedicate this book to every person fighting an invisible illness. I have learned in the past nineteen years while fighting my own battle that others barely have sympathy for what they can see, let alone for what they cannot. You are stronger than you realize. Life really is one step at a time even if you feel like the next step will be your last. Keep fighting that faithful fight and keep smiling. My hope is that this book brings you to a place where you feel known and understood.

CONTENTS

PREFACE

There is a list a mile long of the invisible illnesses in our world—some that I have heard of, some that are foreign to me, and two that I unfortunately know too well. My personal battle has to do with endometriosis and infertility. Throughout this book, I am going to take you on my journey from when my pain began to the present. In the year this was written, I turned thirty years old. I have a lot left to my story throughout my life that is unwritten as yet. However, I feel like I have gone through experiences that some do not see in their entire lifetime, and I felt a tugging on my heart to share my story with you.

Looking back over the years, there is a lot that I wish was different for me, but it made me so much stronger. It sounds cliché, and I never thought I would be the person reflecting and honestly saying that I would not be the same if I did not go through the hills and valleys. In my book you are going to hear about a wide variety of topics. I hope if there is a piece of my journey that you can relate to, that it brings you to a place of feeling known and understood. There were too many times throughout my struggles where I felt like not a single soul on the planet could truly understand the depth of where I was coming from, and it terrified me.

I want this book to be the change for you so that when you open it, you realize that someone out there can relate. You are not alone in your pain. The struggle with invisible illnesses is that we do not talk about them enough. We bottle them up inside and try to deal with issues on our own. People need people. We are all human beings with basic instinct needs. You will never believe the impact when you start sharing your story. I found so many others like me when I began to open up, and I pray that one day that is the same for you. That being said, let us dive in together on this crazy rollercoaster of my own personal "faithful fight."

ACKNOWLEDGMENTS

If it were not for the unwavering and unfailing love of Jesus Christ, I would never be where I am emotionally and mentally today. I learned that His promises will always shine through even during my darkest days. While the love and support from others might be fleeting at times, He never left my side once.

Thank you to my husband, Chris, for showing up to every doctor's appointment, researching with me, and always having a listening ear available for when I needed you. I dedicate this as well to all my family members who believed in me and helped to guide me through the hard and unbearable times. To my forever friends, thank you for never making me feel like an outcast and always embracing me with open arms just as I am. I love you all.

1

The Doctor Who Believed Me

There are not many more infuriating feelings in this world than knowing in your gut you are 100 percent without a doubt right about something, yet no one believes you. Granted, the stubbornness that correlates with that at times can get in the way of one being correct. My personal story dates to when I was twelve years old. It is hard to imagine it has already been nineteen years. To fully understand where someone is currently, it helps to know where they came from. Before we jump to where I am currently in life, I want to take you on a journey through my past.

I grew up with parents who were present. I never once had to wonder if they loved me. I've lost count of the number of times I have heard both parents tell me they are proud of me. Despite their divorce, never once did I go without. Both of my parents worked hard to provide an incredible life for my brother and me. No one is perfect, and mistakes were made, but I knew then and know now that they always did the best they could. The one area that was a little different for me than some of my friends growing up revolved around doctors. My dad is a chiropractor, and I fully believe in chiropractic. Due to this, we were not a family that rushed to the doctor just for any ache and pain. This is not a bash on my parents for not taking me to the doctor sooner—who is to say that a doctor would have found my endometriosis earlier anyway. It is an invisible illness for everyone, including parents.

Throughout my childhood and into my teenage years I played softball. I absolutely loved putting my uniform on and getting out on the field. When tryouts began in third grade for my first Park District team, I joined, and we were asked what position we wanted to play. I always wanted to be the catcher, so I went for it. Other than being used as a utility player my sophomore year of high school, I caught every game I ever played in. My junior year was the last year that I ever played—partially due to the wear and tear on my knees but also due in large part to the pain in my low back and abdomen. I never really told anyone about the second reason for quitting my softball career because the reason behind leaving did not really matter; I was just done. I knew my time was up when a girl ran home from third base, slid into me, and cleated my inner thigh. I dropped the ball and fell over screaming. It hurt and left a mark, but the reality was that it was not nearly as bad as I was making it out to be. I used it as an excuse after that for the reason I wanted out. My body was spent. I was tired physically and mentally. I never stepped foot on a softball diamond after that game.

Part of me does not regret it, and part of me wishes I could have been honest back then about the reason I gave up. But how do you tell people that you want to be done with something that has consumed your life for years because of something they could not see? In my mind, the physical bruising made it easier for them to understand, and they did. My parents never once questioned me after that game. I told them my knees cracked every time I crouched down, and they could see the bruising on my body, and for them, that was enough. So, I was good with it.

After high school graduation at the age of eighteen, I finally convinced my parents that I needed to see a doctor. Never did I think postgraduation, while my friends were enjoying summer, that I would be researching gastrointestinal doctors. Quite frankly, I'd never even heard of a gastrointestinal doctor. My stomach pains had me laid up in bed, canceling plans with friends and family, and questioning if it was all in my mind. It was time for my first colonoscopy. First, whoever created a colon cleanser had to have gone through some things in life because I am convinced that their goal was to make people's lives miserable. The words *disgusting, nauseating,* and just plain *nasty* come to mind.

Anyway, I drank it and showed up to the hospital for my procedure. I got my first IV during this time—thank you, God, for great veins! This also meant it was my first time going under anesthesia. The doctor looked at me in the room and told me it was going to feel like a bee sting. At that point I began to get extremely nervous because who really wants to be stung by a bee? That was all I remembered until I woke up. Before I left the hospital, the doctor came in the room and said, "Everything was clear. We did not find anything. You are good to go." I just stared at him thinking, *I'm sorry. You found nothing? How is that possible? I am in pain! There has to be something on the scan. Last time I checked, bowel movements ending in copious amounts of blood*

3

are not normal. This in no way was going to help anyone in my life believe my pain.

A year went by, and the pain got worse, but I kept trying to live life the best I could. I transferred from the community college near my home to the University of Wisconsin-Whitewater. It was far enough away from home to where I felt like I was finally an adult, doing life on my own, but it was close enough for those times I wanted to be a kid again and see my parents. College was going great—I met a ton of amazing people who remain in my life to this day, and I had a roommate who became one of my best friends. I was a solid two months into my new adult life before I called my mom crying. As I told her, something just was not right.

I woke up one October morning and climbed out of my lofted bed. As soon as my feet hit the ground, I screamed in agonizing pain. Obviously, the first thing I did was call my mom because even from ninety miles away she could make it all better. She told me to take two Advil, take a nap, and call her when I woke up. We now look back and joke about her response because it was such a typical response for my mom. So, I did what she told me because mother knows best. After I woke from my nap, I could barely take a breath without feeling jabbing pain in my side. I called my roommate who was in class and told her I needed her to take me to the emergency room. Being the amazing person she is, she left class to drive me twenty minutes to the nearest ER. It could have been her using me as an excuse to get out of class early, but I like to think it was her just being a kind soul.

Forty-five minutes and three different tests later, it was determined that my appendix was about to rupture. I did not have any time to process what was happening. I got wheeled into the operating room, and next thing I knew, I was awake in my room with three incisions in my stomach and a few pounds lighter. My parents and a couple of friends dropped everything they were doing to drive there and be with me. My roommate took care of me the next two weeks when I could not even walk to the bathroom alone. I learned in this moment who my people were—more to come on that later.

The big question I kept asking myself after surgery was, *What makes an appendix rupture on a healthy nineteen-year-old girl who was cleared by a doctor one year ago?* At my postop appointment, the doctor said that the cause was probably from something I ate with seeds in it and to stay away from anything with seeds for a while. So, by avoiding everything bagels and banana peppers, maybe my pain would just evaporate as quickly as my appendix did?

My college years were incredible. I learned so much and met people who changed my world for the better and some who changed it for the worse. But as I've discovered, those groups of people make us who we are. I graduated with a bachelor's in business administration with a degree in entrepreneurship in 2012 and got lucky enough to meet my now husband during my time spent at Whitewater. I feel blessed for the opportunities that college provided for me, and I would not have changed any of it even if I could. All the experiences shaped me into who I am today, and without each of them, who knows what my life would look like now.

After college, I moved to Madison, Wisconsin, to take the first job opportunity that came my way. I knew all of two people who lived there and was in a foreign city that I went to visit one time prior to signing my apartment lease. I did take day trips throughout my senior year in college to a town just outside of Madison, but that was for voluntary doctor's appointments. These appointments were ones that I signed up for. Rewind to a few months back from graduation. You see, I was a very fortunate girl who had parents that paid for my schooling, but I was on my own for my extra spending money. So, I got a job, and that paid for my fun nights out and a little extra here and there, but it was not enough to put away a decent savings. So, after some heavy research, I found this facility near Madison that specialized in infertility treatment. Egg donations paid a lot of money, and I have always been the kind of person who is ready to help anyone in need. What better way to help a couple that has been struggling to start a family than to give them the baby they have always wanted, all while making great money? It was a win/win for me. Never in a million years would I have guessed that this would be the doctor who would eventually believe all my pain.

At this time in my life, in early 2012, I had heard of infertility, but I did not know anyone who went through it. I was in my senior year of college, and after class a couple of days a week, I would drive from Whitewater to Madison for doctor's appointments to see if I qualified to be an egg donor. I passed the medical clearance and the psych evaluation. This was the first time I was faced with the process of what is entailed with infertility treatment. Although I was not treating myself, I needed to produce as many eggs as possible. So, at the age of twenty-one, I left the doctor's office with more medications than I had ever seen in my life. It still amazes me that the process for this includes just handing over large dosages of medication and trusting that the person is doing these injections properly.

After three months of prep, it was time for my final shot and egg retrieval. I went into the doctor's office, had a dose of anesthesia, and the next thing I knew I woke up in recovery. I will never forget the look on the doctor's face when I woke up. She looked mad and almost as if she was disgusted with me. She reminded me how much money the parents in this case were paying and asked me if I understood. Very confused, I looked at her and confirmed that I knew everything she was saying. I asked her what the issue was, and she said that she questioned if I took any of the medicine. I showed her every bruise all over my body. I asked her what made her think this? She told me there was not a single egg they could retrieve. Everyone left the office that day feeling very confused. I was heartbroken after this because I knew that the parents had to pay all that money—I received my check, and they did not receive a baby. It is an extremely flawed system.

A few weeks postprocedure had passed, I was now officially a college graduate, and my move to Madison was in the works. However, I could not get the look on the doctor's face out of my mind. I called up the facility and wanted an answer as to how everything could have transpired if I followed directions for the donation perfectly. She was willing to run some tests on me to see if we could get an answer. Just as with all my medical tests in the past, every single one of them came back normal. Obviously, something had to be wrong, and for once I had a doctor that agreed. The answer could not just be "nothing." So, I went into

7

her office, and she said she thought the explanation for everything could be summed up in one word: endometriosis. I looked at her and said, "endo what?" Clearly, I had no idea what word just come out of her mouth. She explained to me that endometriosis could be summed up as lesions that would adhere themselves to my insides. They could cause stomach pain, back pain, blood in the stool, exhaustion, and infertility. I have now experienced every symptom she listed, and I received this little glimpse of hope for the first time in a while. No one wants to be diagnosed with anything, but everyone deserves answers to not be made to feel crazy. I asked her what antibiotic she could prescribe so I could go on my way and get this out of my body. That was when she gave me the second look in our time together that caused my stomach to drop and blood pressure to rise. She informed me it was not that simple. Exploratory surgery would be needed, and if her theory was in fact true, she would need to burn the lesions off. The odds of getting it all in one procedure would be slim to none. I had a long journey ahead of me. All I knew was that I wanted answers, so I agreed to go forward with the surgery.

The obstacle of endometriosis is that it is invisible on every test out there unless you get opened under the knife. Ironically, she also said that if she was right, she fully believed that my appendix was not going to rupture back when I'd had it removed. She believed that the ER doctors did not have expertise in endometriosis, and there was a good chance that my appendix was swollen from lesions and not from anything to do with seeds. So, I guess the bright side in all this was that everything bagels could be put back into my diet.

The only view of an operating room that I ever had up to this point was from all the medical television shows that I was addicted to. The doctor wheeled me into the operating room after I kissed my family, and I was terrified. The double doors opened, and everything smelled like bleach and metal. It was freezing cold. All I could think of was backing out, but I knew it was too late. I fully trusted my doctor, and she grabbed my hand after seeing the fear in my eyes and told me, "I got you!" I was having this all done at a teaching hospital, but it never crossed my mind what that truly meant. The anesthesiologist told me that he had a student in the room with him and asked if I was okay with this student putting the tube down my throat once I was out. I remember widening my eyes in this moment and thinking, *You have got to be kidding me.* I asked the doctor if he would be standing there making sure he did it properly, and with a chuckle in his voice, he said, "Absolutely." I responded, "Okay, but he better not mess up." Everyone in the room laughed, and out I went.

This laparoscopic exploratory surgery was supposed to last forty-five minutes. When I woke up, my mom was in the room crying, and I was so confused because I thought I was only out for less than an hour. Little did I know this forty-five-minute procedure lasted almost five hours. When the doctor got inside, she noticed more lesions than ever expected. She came into the recovery room and let me know that if I did not get that procedure done, I would have needed a kidney transplant within a year. I was diagnosed with stage four advanced endometriosis. My entire insides were covered in lesions. She was able to burn off most of them during the five hours, but there were some she was not able to get to. I was filled with so many emotions, due in part to the side effects of waking up from anesthesia. I was so relieved to finally have answers. I did not wish that anything was severely wrong with me, but I did want them to find something—anything. I did not want to go through all this just to wake up and the doctors tell me that all was perfect because I knew my pain was not imaginary. This finally solidified that I was not crazy and making all the pain up.

I spent a lot of time postsurgery researching endometriosis. Prior to being diagnosed, I never heard of the word. But afterward, it was like this word was popping up all over the place. I heard radio stations discussing advertisements, television commercials talking about studies, and even multiple celebrities talking about their own struggle with the disease. Just because the lesions were burned out during surgery did not mean that it was gone forever. Some lesions remained, and some were bound to grow back over time. My low back pain also did not subside despite most of the lesions being gone. I was so thankful and blessed to have met a doctor that believed me and was prepared to help me get whatever treatment I wanted. However, what I did not know was that I was going to be one in four who would experience infertility years down the road due to endometriosis.

So, now I had the doctor that believed me, but what would lie ahead would be the treatment that tested me—treatment for endometriosis and ultimately treatment for infertility. What I thought was the end after the diagnosis was only the beginning of a gut-wrenching, traumatizing, and mentally draining journey.

2

The Treatment That Tested Me

When you are a twenty-two-year-old woman, a lot of hopes and dreams can fill your mind. You wish for moments and memories that you can take with you forever. What you never prepare for is to hear your doctor say that your next step is to be put into menopause. In my mind, there was a whole life that was to be lived in between graduating college and menopause. Perhaps travel the world, get married, raise a family, start a career ... just to name a few. Menopause was supposed to come *after* the goals and dreams, not before. My mom barely scratched the surface of that stage in life, so it was extremely unfair to me that I had to experience the side effects that came along with menopause at such a young age. Regardless of my feelings, my doctor had my best interest at heart. She said that this next step would be the least invasive and give me the best chance at feeling better, so menopause it was.

Right before I was about to start treatment for my endometriosis by using medication, I had an episode one night where I felt extremely sharp pain on my right lower abdomen. I decided to take myself to the emergency room after it hurt to breathe. I remembered the whole appendix of 2009 situation and did not want this to be another "rush into surgery fiasco," so I went sooner this time. I had a scan done in the ER where they found a cyst on my right ovary. The doctor came in and told me words that no one ever wants to hear. "You know, this could mean cancer, right?" I lost it. I was in the ER by myself, and this doctor, who I'd never met before, without an ounce of care in his voice, just dropped the C word. I broke down hysterically to the point where I could not breathe, and he just kept talking. I finally looked at him and yelled, "*Stop!* I'm not sure who you think you are, but you do not just drop a sentence like that and continue to talk without letting someone process your words." It was the first time in my life I can remember sticking up for myself and advocating for my treatment. He clearly felt bad; you could see it in his face that he knew he messed up. I told him I wanted a copy of the scan, and I wanted to be discharged.

The next week or so consisted of me trying to process everything that I'd heard. At the end of the day, this was just another doctor not knowing anything about endometriosis and saying mindless medical terms without anything to back it up. I had a cyst that was rupturing. That was it—nothing more, nothing less. I took a step back and realized that the invisibility of this disease was not going to break me. Every ache and pain was going to drive me up the wall unless I took a deep breath and just took it day by day. The plan prior to this ER visit was to do the surgery (check) and then do the medication. So, it was time for the next step in this journey.

I started to see a doctor at a treatment facility in Madison where they could administer the medicine injections into my side. The injections were given to me twice throughout a six-month time frame. Some warnings I was given were to expect headaches, sensitivity to light, exhaustion, and hot flashes. Everything a twenty-something wants, right? Wrong! It was horrible. Thinking back over the years of all I have been through, this stage in my life was surprisingly the easiest. However, amid it all, I wanted out. I wanted to crawl out of my own body. For months, every single night was a struggle to sleep. I was uncomfortable on a completely new level. And, to add insult to injury, at the end of the day, I do not think the medication helped me at all. Every person is different, and you must do what is right for you; what works for some might not work for others. For me personally, it is not that I wish I did not do it; I just do not think the benefit outweighed the pain I suffered during the process. What the medication did teach me, though, was who had my back and who did not give up when the going got hard. I was an exceptionally tough person to be around during those injections. My mood swings were out of control. I did not know what would make me happy. I became an indecisive, angry, emotional rollercoaster of a human being. If I were able to walk away from me, I would have. The people who I thought would be in my life forever started drifting away from me, and my job became a struggle day in and day out.

Without getting too much into it, because quite frankly the depth of this next piece is for a book of a different type, it was time for me to leave Madison. I had another episode a bit more extreme than the last where I ended up in the ER; I felt alone and misunderstood by everyone surrounding me and needed a support system greater than the one I had at the time. Home was where my family was, and I needed to be closer to them. So, I quit my job, broke my apartment lease, packed up, and within a few weeks was living back in Illinois with my mom and stepdad. Surgery was done, medication shots were done, and yet I had no relief. I did some research and found a world-renowned endometriosis specialist in Illinois.

I made an appointment with this doctor and spent about four months in and out of his office. He would run tests and sometimes meet with me. No legitimate treatment but more so just observing me. There was one incident where he never saw me. His nurse came into the office and asked me how I had been feeling, and I told her I was experiencing extreme low back pain and exhaustion all the time. I had an examination done and got a bill in the mail a few weeks later. It was for the office visit, exam, and $250 for a mental evaluation. I called the doctor's office and asked them what that last charge was for. They said it was because the nurse documented that she talked to me about my mental health. I told the billing department that all she did was ask one casual question. After a battle on the phone for what seemed like hours, the charge was dropped. That should have been my major red flag to leave this doctor's office for good, but due to my current state of desperation, I stayed.

At this point, about eight months had gone by since my exploratory surgery. I felt even worse than before. My entire insides hurt. A scan that this expert doctor did revealed that I had a tilted uterus. He said that it would not cure my endometriosis, but there was potential that a uterine uplift could reduce some of my daily pain. He added that in addition to this procedure, he could clip the presacral nerve to essentially eliminate the pain in my low back. He did warn me that this clipping does not always work. I was on the fence about whether I wanted this done because if at the end of the day it was not going to cure me, did I really want to put my body through another procedure, recovery, and more scar tissue? After much debate, I decided it was my best option for progressing toward a better future.

The surgery was set for one week prior to my start date at the first corporate job I'd secured. It could not have come at a worse time because the last thing I wanted was to be the new hire in my first *big girl* role in life that looked weak or that people would have a reason to judge right off the bat. But timing at this point in my life was not always in my favor, so why start now? At least this was one way to get over my people-pleasing tendencies.

It was time to get rolled into my third operating room in five years. My appendix had been taken, endometriosis had been diagnosed, and now it was time for my uterine uplift and clipping of my presacral nerve. These procedures went smoothly ... or at least I thought they did at the time. The doctor took a fairly short time in the operating room, and this time brought my mom to tears for a different reason. He went into the waiting room to tell her that the procedure was finished, and he had great news to report. My stage four advanced endometriosis went down to a stage one. There were hardly any lesions inside of me anymore at this point. In fact, he said it was nothing short of a miracle and that this could be, "only God." There was a bright side to this

15

whole situation after all. So, you might be asking yourself, what was the issue? Everything sounds great! It was not great at all.

The first sign of an issue postsurgery was when I sneezed for the first time. I figured the pain in my lower abdomen was probably because I just had a laparoscopic surgery, so I really thought nothing of it. Fast-forward a few months. Every sneeze, every cough felt like a knife was being stabbed into my abdomen. When I was driving, I would have episodes where I physically had to pick my leg up to shift from gas to brake. It was not safe by any means. I would be doing absolutely nothing, and it would be hard to catch my breath with the pain. If I complained about the pain to certain family members, the response would be an eye roll or comments along the lines of, "Oh, you are fine" or "What's wrong now?" I certainly did not have many compassionate people in my life at this point. I could count on one hand the number of people in my corner that *showed* they cared for my pain. I was being made to feel crazy, and I even began to feel like maybe this was all phantom pain because I was used to being internally hurt for so long.

The last thing I wanted to do was run back to the doctor for them to tell me that this was just the healing process. There was no way this sharp pain was a part of this process. I felt like I was not getting what I needed from this "world-renowned" surgeon, especially from a bedside manner perspective. If I would have posted this doctor's review online, he would not have a job. He completely ruined the inside of my body. I found another doctor in my area that was an OBGYN but had expertise in endometriosis. There was no harm in making an appointment with him for a second opinion on this pain. He ended up being an angel sent directly from heaven. I have never had a doctor before him or after him who cared the way he did. He never once made me feel just like another number. He and his nursing staff made me feel heard and understood.

During my first appointment with him, I explained all about the doctor that I saw a few months prior and the procedures that he performed, including the painful symptoms that had developed since. He needed to test his theory through some scans, but he believed the issue was that the knot that was tied during the uterine uplift was done incorrectly and was causing me this severe pain. Lo and behold, he could not have been more correct. A uterine uplift is done by detaching the uterus, lifting it up, and then reattaching/anchoring it to the muscle inside of your abdomen. When the right-sided knot was tied off, this surgeon tied it incorrectly causing stabbing and uncontrollable pain. I was filled with so much anger because I wanted to be pain free, and my body was not having it. I was in pain due to uncontrollable and now *controllable* circumstances for years. Thankfully, my new angel of a doctor took me in for my fourth surgery to fix what was broken. I kid you not, despite being minutes out of surgery; I was in less pain in recovery than I was for the months preceding this fix.

I considered suing Dr. World Renowned for his mishap, but at the end of the day I knew my attorney fees would be outrageous. I was twenty-four years old at this point, living at home, and working a successful job, but there was no way despite my success that I would be able to beat him in a malpractice suit. There was probably a chance, but the stress of hiring attorneys and paying them my full check to fight him—someone who had accreditations from all over the world—felt like a losing case before it even started. So, I did what I thought was right at the time and just moved on. To make matters worse, the clipping of the presacral nerve did not even work. It was supposed to alleviate my low back pain issues. In his defense, which you will not hear me say often, he warned me that there are cases where the clipping does not work on some patients. Lucky me, I was one of those cases. I chose in this moment to be the bigger person and walk away from him and his corrupt office forever. I never saw him again, and I ended up in the hands of an incredible doctor who never once failed me. He fixed me up, believed in me, and supported me throughout the next three years.

After leaving Illinois and moving to Wisconsin when I married my husband, I stayed with my doctor. I would come back to do my yearly visit with him, but unfortunately it got to the point where I was told another specialist would be needed, and this time, he could not help me. Now, instead of treating for endometriosis as I had been for years, I was sadly being referred out to meet with an infertility specialist. My doctor in Illinois was able to do preliminary work with me, but it got to the point where my needs far outweighed his specialty. I was treated under his care during the full year that I used Clomid to try and help get pregnant. He did some scans of my tubes to test them. The scans all came out perfectly, which proved to be ironic as my journey continued. Yet, nothing seemed to be working. It was time to say goodbye to him and begin care with an infertility specialist in Wisconsin. Treatment with them was nothing like I had ever imagined women going through. Now, I was about to become a statistic as I began my infertility treatment.

My husband and I tried to get pregnant naturally for one full year. The Clomid did not work, so our next step was to try intrauterine insemination (IUI). This was the safest route to take before going into full-blown in vitro fertilization treatment (IVF). Circling back to my year of Clomid treatment, this was relatively easy compared to the other pieces in the journey. However, while in it, it was excruciating. This pill-form medication resulted in headaches like I have never experienced in my entire life. I felt like I could not hold my head up without it exploding. It gave me overwhelming compassion for anyone who gets chronic migraines. They seemed to express similar symptoms, and I never knew their pain. I would not wish these headaches on anyone, ever. That was the physical frustration, but more so was the emotional toll this piece of treatment took on me. I was told these pills could help to get me pregnant. But every month, disappointment was thrown in my face. One day late, and I would get so excited, until a trip to the bathroom would prove me wrong yet again. All the while, it seemed like everyone around me was getting pregnant. I felt broken. My endometriosis was a disease that affected me but not really those around me. This time my infertility was disappointing so many around me. Comments were being made left and right by friends and family members about when my husband and I would have children. Most did not know our struggle because I did not want to include them when they really could care less about my other struggles in life, so why include them now? I did not want more hurtful comments to come out of their mouths, so instead I just pushed my feelings deep down inside of me and hid them the best I could.

As I stated before, the Clomid failed us, so IUI was next on the planning docket. This was the first time I really got to understand the phases in their entirety of infertility. As I grew up and would hear about the need for assistance in getting pregnant, I never realized how many steps took place before IVF was attempted in most cases. IUI is most simply described as injecting the sperm into the uterus to bypass other areas to give the little guys a shorter distance to swim to reach an egg. I was under the impression that this step would require little to no effort. We would just show up, my husband would give his donation, and we would be out of there and on our way to growing our family. Once again, I was wrong. We had to go through so many rounds of testing prior to the actual procedure. I had a ton of blood work done, ultrasounds, and other various scans. My husband also needed to be tested. To our surprise, there were some levels off in his testing. The doctor liked what she saw for the most part, but there were numbers that were not reaching the level she would have liked to see.

Chris had to make an appointment with their urologist before we continued the process to make sure there was not anything serious going on. At this point I had coped with the fact that I had so many issues wrong with my insides that nothing really surprised me anymore. What broke my heart in these next few weeks was the look of discouragement in my husband's eyes. He did not want to add to the reason that our family was not growing yet; nobody would ever choose to be put in that position. After many tests, he was cleared, and we were able to go through with our first round of IUI.

On my way to the doctor's office, I did the only thing I knew would make me feel less stressed—I stopped for a bagel. In case you were wondering, it was asiago cheese with salmon cream cheese to be exact. There is just something about bagels that ease my stomach and calm my fears. Crazy, I know, but I promise they work wonders. Also, how ironic is it that the food items that I once was told could have been the cause of my pain with the seeds was the food bringing me comfort? Sorry, where was I? Oh yes, on my way to the doctor's office for the big day. Only the best swimmers were injected before the two-week wait began. They tell you not to take pregnancy tests before the two weeks are up because the accuracy could be extremely flawed. I genuinely felt like this was the longest two weeks of my life. It was time for my blood test, and I could not wait for the results. The phone rang, and my heart sank. Could this be it? I have a pretty good sense of how to read people based on their tone of voice. As soon as I heard the nurse, I knew this was not our time. "It's negative," she said. So, after many tears and a few deep breaths, I gathered myself and had to prepare for the next steps.

Round two of IUI was now scheduled for three weeks later. Despite the clearance from my husband's doctor, there were still some numbers issues with his sperm. My doctor said trying one more round of IUI could not hurt us before beginning IVF. The day had come for the procedure. I was driving to the doctor's office and had to make a pit stop; I needed a bagel, of course. As I pulled out of the parking lot to make my trek to the doctor, my phone rang; it was their office. I instantly knew something was wrong. There was no reason they needed to be calling me when my appointment was in thirty minutes. The nurse always calls on behalf of the doctor, but this time, it was the doctor herself calling. Now I knew there was definitely something wrong. She explained that after separating the useable sperm from the nonusable, not enough good ones were left to be able to do the procedure. So, round two of IUI was canceled.

My husband felt devastated that because of him, we could not go through with this round. He watched me suffer in pain with the prep leading up to this point, and it was all for nothing. I did my best to reassure him that this one single setback was not the only contributing factor to our struggles. He was so supportive through every step, and now it was my time to support him. There were many situations in this journey so far that allowed our relationship to grow stronger when it could have been destroyed. This was just another scenario to add to our list. Our doctor met with us and explained that at this point she felt the best thing we could do for ourselves was begin the IVF process. So, we did just that.

What should have been an eight- to ten-week process lasted over a year for us. Every patient's story is different. What I learned during this time was that one person's amount of pain does not negate another's. Physical, mental, and emotional pain is handled differently by everyone. When you sit in the waiting room and look around, everyone's story is completely different as to how they got to where they are at and to where they are going. However, one thing we all have in common is the level of understanding that it takes to come alongside another person facing these struggles. Unless you are going through it, grasping the true understanding of the pain and struggle is nearly impossible. The date was February 10, 2019, and the injections were beginning. Our days were now filled with needles, medicine, pain, emotions, and uncertainty.

Depending on what doctor you treat with, the medications given can vary. I think that is a part of this whole journey that is a bit frustrating to me. If I treat with facility A, my treatment plan looks completely different than if I treated with facility B down the road. Some doctors prep with birth control, while others avoid it at all costs. At the end of the day, it is all about how you advocate for yourself and do your own research. If you ever feel like you do not trust a decision being made, you must speak up. Unfortunately, we live in a world where not all doctors have your best interest at heart, and some are just money hungry for your business. It is a sad reality of our society. Like I have said, I have a pretty good gut reaction to reading people, and if I ever feel like something is not right, I act on it. In my personal situation, after being royally mistreated by Dr. World Renowned in years past, I never let that happen again. The care I was under at this point for IVF was with a group of women doctors who made me feel heard and understood. I fully trusted them.

The medications they prescribed me were Lo Loestrin Fe, Leuprolide, Gonal-F, Menopur, Pregnyl, and Progesterone in Oil. I was called by the specialty pharmacy that all the medication would be arriving to my home. When I tell you that the size of this box was ginormous, it is not an exaggeration. I could not believe my eyes when I opened this box up. Bags of needles, gauze pads, alcohol swabs, and medical waste bins accompanied the medication. I felt like I had a hospital inside of my home. It was truly mind-blowing to me that when you sign up for this portion of infertility treatment that the process includes shipping loads of medication to your home and entrusting you to give yourself the medication properly. My husband and I both went to business school and felt extremely unqualified for this task.

Pills began, alongside daily injections. I am normally someone who bruises very easily. Surprisingly, none of these shots caused too many bruises for me. I know not everyone is as lucky. The piece that did not go very well for me was the side effect of light sensitivity. My job required me to be around florescent lights most of the week, and I have never felt more defeated in my life. I physically could not look at my computer without wanting to vomit. I made a request for some sort of assistance to get the lights out of my eyes so that I could do my job without extreme pain. They were less than helpful for weeks until finally I told facilities to just remove the lights above me. This helped tremendously. Besides this annoyance, the prep period prior to egg retrieval was not as tolling as I had anticipated. Sure, at times, it was emotionally brutal; but looking back, I think I handled it like a champion.

A few weeks passed, and it was time for my baseline ultrasound. Leading up to this, my stomach felt pain and sensitivity, but I had assumed it was from the needles poking me daily. Unfortunately, a 23 cm cyst was found on my ovary. IVF had to be put on hold for a few weeks for the cyst to hopefully shrink. It was now the beginning of April 2019, and we were given the clearance for shots to start back up again. We awaited the next ultrasound to see if we could continue further with injection treatment this round. Finally, for the first time in who knows how long, we were able to leave the doctor's office with happy tears instead of sad and disappointing ones. The cyst was completely gone, and I was given the green light to up the medication. My world was now going to consist of three shots every night, along with going to the doctor every two days, inclusive of ultrasounds and blood draws.

The day was finally here—egg retrieval day. All the prep and obstacles led to this day, and we were full of so much excitement, anxiety, and anticipation. Prior to going under, I was told I had sixteen follicles on my right ovary and eleven on my left. Of the twenty-seven, thirteen of them were considered "matured." A "mature" follicle means that it is measuring past the size that they like to see for good, strong growth. What is one more hurdle to jump through beforehand, though? As the anesthesiologist was trying to get the IV in so the procedure could begin, he missed four times. I wanted to get dressed and run out of the procedure room and just call it quits. I was so frustrated. The fifth time proved to be the charm, though, and under anesthesia I went to wait for the outcome.

Nineteen, yes, you read that right, nineteen eggs were retrieved. We were over the moon excited. I kept repeating the number back to the doctor because I literally could not believe it. However, just because nineteen were retrieved did not mean all of them would be fertilized. I liked our chances though. The phone rang, and the answer was in. Eight of the nineteen fertilized successfully! However, only three of those eight were able to be used for transfers due to them reaching the blastocyst stage of development. In layman's terms, this meant we had three chances of having biological children. We decided we would do a day five fresh transfer with our first embryo and freeze the other two to be transferred at later dates. The difference between these two is that a day five fresh transfer means the embryo never reaches a frozen state before the transfer is made after five days of maturity, whereas a frozen embryo would need to be thawed before the transfer occurs.

Two days before our transfer date was scheduled, the phone rang yet again. At this point I was so sick of the doctor's office calling when I was not expecting it. It was never good news. Much to my surprise, this call was not as bad as I expected. She said that the embryo was developing faster than anticipated, and they wanted us to do a day three fresh transfer versus the scheduled day five. So, on April 28, 2019, our first baby was transferred into my uterus. I have debated internally about how to share what came next. I feel like I owe it to my baby to share the full story of what unfolded in the next chapter instead of looping the story into this treatment section. The spoiler alert and extremely short version is that the transfer was successful but devastatingly ended in tragedy. You will have to read ahead to unveil the depth of this story.

Fast forward, it is now September 2019, and we have been given the clearance to proceed with our second embryo transfer; first frozen. More needles and medication were reintroduced into my body in prep for this piece of the journey. My body was ready, and ultrasounds showed perfect lining levels to proceed. On October 21, 2019, our second baby was transferred into my uterus. Blood work came back ten days later, and it was positive. I owe the same respect to my second baby as I do my first to share what unfolded after this positive transfer in the next chapter as well. My second one did not consist of the same gut-wrenching experiences as the first, but the ending was the same. After two successful transfers, we still ended up without a baby in our arms.

We have our third and final frozen embryo still left for a transfer at this point in the story. My biggest concern was that after everything we had been through, I wanted to make sure that at the end of the day we could look back and know that we did absolutely everything we could to grow a biological family. My doctor scheduled a hysterosonogram, HSN for short. This is the action of having an ultrasound done but with a catheter inserted and saline solution injected into the uterus to make sure there are not any foreign bodies calling my uterus its home and thus accepting but then quickly rejecting my pregnancies. Luckily, the scan was perfect. In fact, she called my insides beautiful. Therefore, I am literally beautiful on the inside and outside. It has been confirmed. This final piece in my infertility journey closes an almost double-decade-long gap of all the pain and suffering I endured. You will have to make your way to the end of this book to see what came next.

Looking back and reading through this chapter, it still amazes me the amount of treatment that it takes to fight internal disorders such as endometriosis and infertility. You never know the battles that people face. I have grown immensely after being forced to face these struggles. I encourage everyone to give people some grace. Sharing struggles does not come easy to everyone; in fact, it does not come easy to the majority. It is easier to say you are fine and all is good instead of sharing the depth of your physical, mental, or emotional pain. Most cannot understand the struggle and you feel like it is not worth it to try to get them to come alongside of you. The more we discuss our internal diseases, the less foreign they will become. Hopefully, together we can change the mind-set of the less empathetic population that exists in our world. With all that being said, that gives you some insight into all the treatment that tested me. Next, you will get a better understanding of all the losses in my life that left me devastated.

3

The Losses That Devastated Me

The problem with loss in our society is that it is perceived with an unspoken expectation that you will miss out on the past and all that comes along with the "what was." However, what I have learned in recent years is that loss exposes us to miss out on the future and the "what could have been." When you lose a loved one, you do not only lose the memories; you lose the imagination of the unknown future. I spoke earlier about two of my babies that I lost and mentioned that they were owed their full stories to be told with a fresh start instead of looping in my experiences with each of them toward the end of a chapter. Here I would like to introduce the world to the two that my husband and I call Raspberry and Cranberry.

First, is our Raspberry. I refer to Raspberry as the stubborn, hardheaded first child. I feel like I am allowed to say this because I too am the first born in my family, and I imagine we would have been a lot alike. With Raspberry, as stated earlier, I had my transfer done on April 28, 2019. What transpired after this was nothing like I would have ever imagined. I found out on May 10, 2019, that the transfer worked, and for the first time in my entire life, I saw the word "positive" on the pregnancy test. I cannot remember a time before or after that moment that I have ever smiled more. The miracle we had been waiting so long for had finally come true.

Sadly, the story does not end there. Five days later, on May 15, 2019, I got a call from the doctor's office that my HCG levels had gone down, and I was told that I miscarried. HCG stands for human chorionic gonadotropin, which is the hormone detected in the body when an embryo is present. A rollercoaster of emotions does not even scratch the surface of what I was feeling in those days. I did my best to cope with my new reality. I was just extremely glad that I did not react too quickly and share my good news with too many people. The last thing I wanted to do was disappoint those around me, which in hindsight was a bit backward in that while I was going through this tragedy, I was still concerned about how others might feel.

I was required to go in for more blood draws until my levels fell below five. So, in for another test I went a week later fully expecting it to be close to negative—but to my surprise, it was not. Instead, my numbers more than tripled three times over and shot up to the mid-700s. My doctor called me and said this was extremely abnormal. Numbers do not just slowly drop and then shoot up out of nowhere; that is not how the body is supposed to work. Then again, my body had not acted "normal" in years, so why start now? She had me come in for an ultrasound so that she could try to see what was going on. I had another blood draw done before my visit, and my numbers surpassed the one-thousand mark. The only thought that kept popping into my mind was that

I could be one in a million where the numbers bounce around, but the baby remains healthy. It was the hope I was leaning on.

Unfortunately, during the ultrasound, the doctor looked everywhere, but she could not find the baby. The numbers consistently increasing at this point meant that the baby was growing somewhere inside of me, but it was not in my uterus where it belonged. She looked everywhere but no baby. She saw a small speck on the ultrasound that she thought could have been it, but it was too hard to tell if it was inside my ovary or inside my right fallopian tube. Nonetheless, regardless of where the baby might have been, it was not in my uterus where it needed to be to have a successful pregnancy. At one point I even jokingly said to the doctor, "Even if you are wrong, and it is not in my ovary or tube, and it is just floating in my arm somewhere, it is definitely not in my uterus, right?" To which she confirmed that to be the case. So, I asked her what I needed to do in order to do the healthiest and safest thing for my body. She confirmed that once the baby made its way outside of my uterus, there was no going back. The baby had attached itself to somewhere it was not supposed to be, and that proved to be extremely dangerous for both myself and the baby. The baby would not be able to develop into a healthy human outside of the uterus, and it would also put me at risk for rupturing organs that could lead to death. Neither of these situations would end well, so action had to be taken. The best option I had was to shrink the embryo and stop the cells from growing. My only other choice would have been to let the baby continue to grow and have my insides broken apart until I rolled the dice to see if I would bleed out and die. It was a no-brainer decision, but nonetheless one that no one should ever have to face.

Of course, all this happened on a Saturday, meaning that the department at the hospital I would normally be able to go to for a shot of methotrexate was closed. Therefore, a six-hour wait in the emergency room was my only option. After an extremely long and unexpected afternoon, a man wearing what looked like a hazmat suit came into the room with a giant needle. Prior to him entering the room, I asked the nurse if the person who would be administering this drug was experienced. She said without a doubt in her voice, "Yes, it is required to have an experienced physician administer this specific type of drug." Well, the joke was on me, because Hazmat Suit Man had zero experience, which he openly admitted to when I asked him. At this point, I was so exhausted and mentally numb that I really didn't care. All he had to do was shoot this giant needle into my right butt cheek; I felt like I could have done it myself. A few moments of stinging and burning later, I was able to leave the hospital. I was told upon discharge that I should expect some minor cramping over the next few days and that the discomfort would be normal. What transpired roughly seventy-two hours later was very far from normal.

On the morning of May 28, 2019, around three o'clock, I started having severe cramping. The pain came and went every few minutes, and when my alarm started to beep around 6:30 a.m., I did my best to get ready for my workday. I remember getting dressed in uncontrollable pain as tears rolled down my cheeks. Finally, after trying to push through it all, my husband said enough was enough, and I was not going into work. Instead, he was taking me to the emergency room. We went to the ER closest to our home. It was luckily a branch of the facility where I did all my infertility treatment, so they had access to all my records. Unfortunately, this was a small ER, and they could only do so much for me at this location. When I walked in and told them I had a confirmed ectopic pregnancy with methotrexate that had been given to me a few days prior, it became all-hands-on-deck.

The concern was that if the methotrexate did not kick in strongly enough yet and the embryo continued to grow, I could be at high risk for bleeding out to the point of death. They administered medications to try to get me to a level of pain where I did not feel like curling in a ball and screaming. They kept adding more medication to the IV, and I continued to get drearier, but the pain on the lower right side was untouched no matter how much medication they pumped into me. This continued for close to seven hours. The ER doctor was in touch with my infertility doctor at the other facility down the road. She was waiting for them to do an ultrasound so she could try to get a better picture of what was going on internally. The hours passed, but they never took me for the scan. Instead, they told me they were clearing a room for me, and I was going to be transferred to their main hospital campus because they wanted me in the hands of someone from this specialty. Since I already had the IV in my arm, I needed to be transported via ambulance.

I arrived at the main campus with two hours to spare before my doctor was going to leave the office for the day. I was now in communication with her, and she told me she ordered the ultrasound and was chart-stalking me awaiting the results. After

33

I got placed into my room, the nurse said to me, "You are here so we can just observe you overnight, and then you can go home." I looked at her like she had three heads. That was not the reason I was there. I told her my doctor had been waiting hours for an ultrasound, and they needed to get me into one before she left for the day. Somewhere between hospitals one and two, communication lines were dropped all over the place, and no one seemed to know what was going on.

I called my doctor and told her the situation. She made a phone call, and within what seemed like minutes, I had a surgeon in my room. He explained to me that at this point regardless of what an ultrasound showed, the best course of action to save my insides and potentially my life was to have surgery to remove the ectopic pregnancy. It did not matter if the ultrasound showed that the embryo stuck to the insides of my ovary, fallopian tube, or my arm (note lighthearted joke above). Regardless, the baby was not in my uterus, and we were now at the point where danger was involved if surgery was not done.

After I got to know the surgeon that would perform the surgery, he informed me that his shift was over in an hour, so a different surgeon would be the one taking my case. I was so drugged up and exhausted at this point I really did not care anymore. I just wanted this entire situation to be over with. Before he left, he asked me one of the hardest yet easiest questions I have ever been presented with. He explained to me that they were 99 percent sure that the embryo was in my right tube, and they were confident they would need to take the entire tube out. He inquired about my left tube and asked me if they noticed anything wrong while they were in there, did I want them to take my left tube out as well. They did not anticipate anything being wrong with the left tube but needed to confirm my wishes. Without hesitating I told him I wanted both tubes out of me. I knew I had two frozen embryos left, did not need my tubes to complete the IVF cycles, and I never again wanted the option of an ectopic pregnancy occurring. If I had the choice to never go through a day like this one again, I was going to make the decision best for my body, my health, and my family.

It was now close to 7:00 p.m. My dad and my stepmom arrived at the hospital just before they were about to wheel me into surgery. My husband walked down to preop with me and sat with me for about fifteen minutes until the anesthesiologist came in to inject that powerful medication of hers. I kissed my husband, and they wheeled me into yet another operating room—hopefully the last one I will need to see for many years to come. I was a bit drowsy, but I remember the surgeon asking me about where I met my husband and me telling her a part of our crazy story centered on college and playing pool. The room of doctors all laughed, and the anesthesiologist put a mask over my mouth and told me to breathe in and count to three. When I got to three, I was not asleep and yelled, "*Stop!* I'm awake." Yet again, the room filled with laughter as she responded, "That was just oxygen. Now you are going to go to sleep; goodnight, Melissa."

I woke up in postop alone with a man sitting next to me. I very groggily asked him who he was. He was a nurse meant to observe me and make sure that my vitals remained stable after coming out of it. Anesthesia affects everyone differently. My most common side effect after surgery is that my bladder spasms despite them draining it during the operation, and I always feel like I must urinate; more to come on that piece in a bit. A side effect that has never impacted me before is itchy eyes. The nurse sitting next to me kept swatting my hand down every time I went to scratch them. Picture this: postsurgery alone, in pain, itchy eyes, and a stranger moving my hand down every time I reached for them. I was a blubbering mess who wanted to punch him but could barely move. I kept crying and asking for my mom and my husband. He said I could not call them, so instead, while the tiles shifted back and forth and my words slurred, I got back at him by calling him a mean, mean man, and then I fell asleep. The next thing I remember I was being wheeled into my room, now surrounded by my husband, dad, stepmom, and my mom and stepdad, who arrived at the hospital during the surgery. It was almost 10:00 p.m. so half of my family left to go home to get some sleep after a long and unexpected night.

My surgeon came into the room to talk with me before I fell asleep to brief me on the surgery. Before she began, I asked her if she could let someone know that I was sorry for calling my postop nurse mean and that I appreciated him protecting me. It was the anesthesia, I promise. Now that we had the apologies and jokes aside, it was time for a serious update. She explained to me that in my right tube was the baby along with two blockages of fluid, so the right tube, as expected, was removed. She showed me pictures and explained that the left tube was found coiled up in a circle and connected itself on the bottom curve to my ovary and the top curve to my uterus. Due to this abnormality, she felt like the safest decision was to remove the left tube as well. She was able to make a clean cut at the bottom of my tube, but the top portion was so entangled and deformed that she had to leave a very small piece attached. If you remember back a few pages, I explained that I had testing done that checked both of my tubes about a year prior to this surgery. Both tubes at that time were in absolute perfect condition. I asked the surgeon what would make a tube go from healthy to coiled up and ultimately defective in one year's time. I appreciated her answer that was full of humility. She said, "I honestly do not know. It is something I have never seen before, and I do not have an answer." Really, it did not matter the reason behind it all because the tubes were gone and were not coming back. It would have been nice to know the "why" for some closure, but this was my new normal, and I just had to accept it. The rest of my family left; my husband went home to get some shut eye, and it was time for me to call it a day—and what a day it was.

Morning came, the sun rose, and a new day had begun. Remember when I told you about my main side effect from anesthesia? This surgery was no different. It was about twelve hours postsurgery, and I knew I needed to urinate, but I could not do it. They eventually had to catheter me after multiple failed attempts. That night they sent me home with a planned postop appointment for one week later, where they said they would remove the catheter. I had a swollen stomach, three incision marks, and a tube with a bag connected coming out of me. Needless to say, I was miserable. Now, it was May 30, the best day in the world— my birthday. This is how I always dreamed of turning twenty- nine—laid up in bed, being served by my husband, and peeing without moving. When worded like that, it does sound like a dream come true perfect way to spend a birthday. To add some sunshine to my gloom, my mom planned on coming over that day to spend time with me. She walked into the room, and standing behind her was the best birthday present I could have ever asked for. My brother, one of my favorite people on the planet, flew in from Arizona and surprised me. Imagine crying hysterically without being able to move your abdominal muscles. It was not a pretty scene, but I was overcome with so much joy seeing him standing there. We sat and talked for hours, and I could not have asked for anything more in that moment.

Day three of having a catheter in, and I was feeling miserable. If they thought that I was going to go four more days with this thing in me, the joke was on them. I called every location of my hospital chain to see who could get me in for a last-minute appointment to remove my catheter. After two hours of phone calls and begging, I found one willing to do it. I unfortunately was not able to drive myself, very few people near me knew of my story, it was a workday, and tracking someone down to take me there was near impossible to find. My very dear friend dropped everything she was doing, came to pick me up, and took me to my appointment. I am forever grateful for her kind and caring heart. The nurse removed the catheter and told me I had one hour to prove I could urinate on my own or else they had to put it back in. Within two minutes, no exaggeration, we had a beautiful waterfall, and she sent me on my merry way. I would not wish a bladder that experiences spasms after a surgical procedure on my worst enemy. It is infuriating.

I am blessed enough to work for a company that allowed me to do my job from home for four weeks to fully recover. The month passed, and my abdomen was healed, but my heart remained broken. I kept having nightmares and flashbacks thinking about the surgeon removing my tube with my baby in it and throwing it in the trash. Days went on, and my life got back to normal, but that piece of me took a long time to recoup from. I do not think I will ever fully be over it. I would not expect anyone to fully move on from that whole situation, so I do not hold myself to any different standard. I am gentle on myself and allow myself to have my hard days of remembrance and reflection.

To my little strong-willed Raspberry: I wish you would have just stayed where you were told to and did not keep pushing on outside of where you belonged, but because of you, I learned a new strength that I did not know I was capable of achieving. I learned contentment, patience, and understanding through your fearlessness. I know you are in Heaven shining down on your daddy and I. Losing you devastated me, but one day we will meet again, and I cannot wait to see you. Until that day, you keep pushing on, and never take no for an answer. I love you always, my first baby.

My next loss story is centered on our second baby, Cranberry. As described in the previous chapter, in September 2019 we were given the clearance to prepare for our second embryo transfer. I was put on birth control for three weeks, followed by Estradiol pills, and eventually progesterone in oil injections. Although it seemed like months of waiting, it was only a few weeks, and we made our way to October 21, 2019; a.k.a. transfer day. I had so much anxiety leading up to this appointment and during it. After the downward spiral from our first try, I never wanted to go through that physical and emotional pain again. However, just like I had done up to this point, I put one foot in front of the other and kept pressing on. A different doctor out of the reproductive center did this transfer. She is incredibly smart, but she lacks people skills. I trust she knows what she is doing, but she in no way ever made me feel comfortable. I could not control that it was her shift that day to cover transfers, so it was what it was. Unlike the first go-around where the doctor pointed everything out on the screen for me to see, did a test run, and then allowed me to ask questions afterward, this time I was in and out in less than ten minutes.

This was the first time I truly understood the cliché behind "mother's intuition." The moment we pulled out of the parking lot, I had a bad feeling about this pregnancy. Even though I knew they transferred the embryo into me, it felt like I was empty, and there was not a baby. I had an overwhelming feeling that the baby was not okay. I toughed out the ten-day waiting period and complied with going into the lab for a blood draw despite my gut feeling. Side note, when I was expecting a phone call with Raspberry, I went into the office to work that afternoon. When I got the call, I hysterically cried at my desk for everyone around me to hear. This time, that was not going to happen. I planned better this time and worked from home. A few hours had passed, and the phone rang. The nurse on the other end of the line shared the news that lo and behold, it was positive. I lacked any emotion out of genuine shock, thanked her, and hung up. I really wanted to be excited and jump for joy, but despite her telling me it was a positive test, it still did not feel real.

I went for my next blood draw forty-eight hours later to confirm that my HCG doubled. It almost doubled but not quite, and the nurse began to grow concerned. So, another two days had passed, and it was time for more confirmation. Another blood draw, and there was the news on November 4, 2019, that I expected all along—the number dropped. She really did not have to tell me because the moment I picked up the phone, I could hear the tone of her voice was less than pleasant—mother's intuition at its finest. She described it to me as a chemical miscarriage. To make matters worse, my HCG was not below five at this point, so even though I knew my baby was not growing, per doctor protocol I had to continue blood draws until it fell below that threshold. I went in for another blood draw, and the phlebotomist had the nerve to say to me, "How many more times are you coming in for this?" To which I felt like responding, "I am sorry I am inconveniencing you; coming into the lab to get a needle poked into my arm is something I actually find fun." I bit my tongue and told her I did not know and went on my way. I had to continue with these draws three more times after that. My numbers finally fell below five, and I was done.

My time with Cranberry was not nearly as dramatic as with Raspberry. There were, however, extreme storms and crazy-looking skies throughout the couple-week time span. My husband likes to imagine that our little Cranberry would have grown up to become a meteorologist. I picture Cranberry as the quiet and shy child—the opposite of its sibling. Cranberry came into our lives and disappeared in the blink of an eye peacefully. The physical aspect of the loss between the two babies may have been different, but the emotional struggle was almost identical. We now had two babies keeping each other company in Heaven, and it was up to us when we would like to proceed with our third and final embryo transfer. We decided to take a couple months off from all treatment to reflect and repair our hearts.

To my shy little Cranberry, you were not with us for very long, but your impact will last a lifetime. When I close my eyes, I picture you loving to be held and comforted—someone who did not speak often, but when you did, you would be full of wisdom. I imagine you to be a lot like your daddy—someone who is okay in the silence and analyzes everything around you. I hope that you and Raspberry are having so much fun playing in Heaven together and keeping each other company. Whenever it storms outside, and the sky is full of crazy clouds and colors, your daddy and I will always take that as you saying "hi" to us. I love you always, my second baby.

My last loss that I would like to share with everyone is dedicated to someone who indirectly relates to my invisible illness struggles. The thing about facing any struggle that people cannot physically see is that sometimes it takes people who will listen to you to help guide you through the pain. When you lose someone who is a part of that circle, you quickly feel like you have no one, even though there are still people who will lend an ear now and then. This is what happened when I lost my grandma Deena. Picture a grandma. If you imagine a sweet, gentle soul who was full of innocence and grace, picture the opposite when you think of my grandma. Do not get me wrong, she loved me with every ounce of her being, but she was not full of that same forgiving love with everyone in her life. She faced a lot of struggles growing up that stuck with her over the years. She was a lifetime New Yorker who was full of opinions and comments about everyone and everything. The things she used to say that annoyed me, I wish to hear one more time. When everyone around her, in her eyes wronged her, I could do no wrong; this bothered a lot of family members, but I loved it. She called me her "Mama Shayna," which to my knowledge can best be described as a Yiddish saying for "pretty girl or beautiful."

Do you have a food or smell that when you are presented with it, it brings you back to a moment in time instantly? That is what I get from minimuffins, tapioca pudding, and dryer sheets. These three things could always be found at Grandma's house. Since my grandma lived in New York and I in the Midwest most of my life, there were a lot of flights taken across the states to be together. Whenever she would pick me up from the airport, without fail, there would be a package of minimuffins with a small bottle of water in the backseat waiting for me. She knew I would need a snack even though our first stop 99 percent of the time was a beeline to the diner. When I would walk into her home, it always smelled like fresh dryer sheets, complimented gracefully with perfect vacuum lines throughout the rooms. And what would a night be without a tapioca pudding cup, while watching old game shows on TV, and me lying on her lap getting my ears tickled with a Q-tip until I fell asleep?

As I grew up and saw her less throughout the years, the

distance never severed our bond. She learned how to text, and I would call her every day after work on my drive home. I was able to share deep issues with her, and she would listen. There were not many, and there still are not many, people that I can share anything and everything with and have them give me a true, honest, listening ear with feedback that I need to hear; and not just what I want to hear. We would clash from time to time, and sometimes a couple days of distance did us good, but no relationship is perfect. She knew about all my endometriosis struggles and only a portion of my infertility due to her being taken away from me without any warning on May 14, 2018.

The day prior was Mother's Day. I spoke to her in the morning, and we had a beautiful conversation. After dinner with our families, my husband gave her a call on our drive home, and I had him tell her that I loved her, and I would call her the next day. The next day never came for her. I went to work like a typical Monday, and all seemed fine in the world. Around 11:30 a.m., I was in the cafeteria heating up my lunch—fettuccini Alfredo, to be exact. As it was warming, I looked down at my phone and saw a text from my mom that read, "Call me now." I never get texts like that from her, so I called her, and she was the most frantic I have ever heard her. She screamed, "Grandma is dead; Grandma is dead; you need to come here right now." I screamed back, "What are you talking about?" Mind you, I was in the center of a cafeteria that seats about one thousand people, two hours away from my mom's home. I grabbed my half-heated lunch out of the microwave and ran over to the table where my coworkers were seated. I was hysterically crying, and my body was convulsing. After about thirty minutes of shaking, I was able to gather myself enough to walk to the car. My amazing coworkers left so that one could drive my car home with me in it, while the other followed. My husband met me at our home, and within twenty more minutes, I had a bag packed and was on the road, going way over the speed limit to get to my mom.

During the drive, I called my uncle who lived in New York at the time. He was at her home, and I needed answers to what happened. To understand the next piece, you will need to know that my grandma was a creature of habit. Every morning she did the same thing in her later years. One of those daily tasks was her going to her local diner to sit and talk with the staff there and help them fill the milk canisters and roll silverware. On this day, she never showed up. Her rituals seemed so odd to some of us, but if not for her habits, who knows how long she would have gone unfound. After she did not show, the staff began to worry. They had one of their sisters go up and down the street they knew she lived on and bang on every door. Once the correct house was found, she made the landlord open the door or else she was going to kick it down. He reluctantly opened it, and there sitting on the couch with her sports radio playing next to her, my beautiful eighty-year-old grandma was found unresponsive. My uncle said that there was a glass of orange juice sitting on the kitchen counter with her vitamins next to the cup. No one knows exactly what happened between the night before when people last heard from her to the afternoon when she was found. But knowing my grandma would never leave something out on the counter for a second longer than it needed to be, our best guess was she woke up that morning, went to take her daily vitamins, did not feel right, and sat down on the couch. That was where her heart stopped. She was taken to the county coroner's office where cause of death was determined to be heart failure. She had no known prior medical issues, aside from arthritis. Sudden heart failure was nothing we saw coming.

After the family gathered at my mom's home in Illinois, the six of us had to decide how we were going to get to New York—and fast because my grandma was Jewish, and in the Jewish religion, they try to bury the next day. At this point it was about 5:00 p.m., and we decided the best bet was to just rent a car and drive, so we did just that. Out of all the people who could have helped make that drive, no one stepped up except me. My only concern was to get us there safely, but the downside to that was that I never got any time to process anything. It was extremely frustrating because my mom was on edge and rightfully so. But because of that, I took the brunt of all her anger with this whole situation. Everyone in the car would make a comment about who knows what, but the second I opened my mouth about anything, I was shot down and made to feel unworthy of speaking. I lost someone too, and for some reason that was not accounted for by a single person in that car. I felt like their personal driver instead of one of the closest people to the one who had passed. Regardless of my feelings, I just kept driving east. About thirteen hours later, we arrived safely. Due to the timing of everything, the funeral was set for May 16, 2018. The crazy, ironic part of this date was that she was supposed to fly out to Illinois to visit that exact day. One of the last voice mails I have saved on my phone from her was from May 3, 2018, and it ends with her saying, "Okay, mommy, so I'm booked for the 16th, ten thirty flight in the morning, beautiful. And I love you, and I'll talk to you later on. I just wanted you to know. Okay, sweetheart, love you, bye." The day and time I should have been seeing her was when we were burying her instead.

Losing her wrecked my life and turned it upside down. After all that I struggled with after her death, I wished for nothing more than to be able to dial her number and vent or to get advice. Most days, even though it is years later, it does not feel real. I find myself driving and wanting to call her, until I remind myself that I cannot. At one point I tried to take a baby step of moving on by deleting her number from my phone, but when I did, all the voice mails I have saved from her changed from her name to just a phone number, so I immediately undid that. She is still on my favorites list, and that is where she will remain forever.

When you are faced with a problem in life, having a support system is incredibly important. You cannot do everything on your own, no matter how tough you think you are. My grandma taught me many life lessons that I will carry with me forever. She had a very hard time trusting people. I learned from her, indirectly and without her knowing it, how important it is to let people in, but not all people. Not everyone deserves to hear your deepest secrets, but knowing who to share with and what to share with them is healthy and a great way to heal past hurts. She is forever loved and so deeply missed. To wrap up the losses that have devastated me before introducing you to the people that have inspired me, I would like to close in a way that she and I would end a lot of text conversations: "I love you times infinity. XOXO Muah."

4

The People Who Inspired Me

I have made multiple mentions up to this point about the "inner circle" and about how people need people. One of the hardest struggles of invisible illnesses is not the pain and is not the doctor's appointments; it is the emptiness of feeling as though you are not understood. The harsh reality is that the people you think are always there for you suddenly disappear as you watch their true colors shine. It becomes apparent when the going gets rough. What I have learned is that many people love me, and they care about my well-being, but they do not know what empathy is. It is not until you release your expectations of people that they lose the ability to keep hurting you. Most of the people in your life are there because you want them to be. You know that they are not malicious, hurtful human beings, or else why would you want them in your life to begin with? Your brain tells you they are good people, but your heart does not understand it. To lose the constant feeling of disappointment begins and ends with you. Believe me, I know it does not seem fair. You are the one suffering physically, mentally, and emotionally, so why should keeping a relationship strong be yet another responsibility to add to your plate? It is because human beings are just that—they are humans. They are imperfect people who will never be able to live up to your needs at every moment of every day.

If you take a step back, you will begin to realize that you can keep every single person in your life that you want there, but it does not mean that you are required to share your deepest and truest feelings with every single one of them. This mind-set will allow your eyes to be opened, and you will begin to fill in your circle. These will be the people that you can go to in good times and in bad. They can rejoice with you when you are in a rejoicing phase, but even more important, they know how to mourn with you when you are mourning. They will not be the ones that talk down to you because you are not feeling like yourself. They will not be the ones who make every conversation about themselves when you need to vent. They will not be the ones who, after years of your suffering, still have no idea what your disease is called. They will not be the ones who give you a hard time for canceling plans. They will not be the ones who do not reach out just to say "hi" after you lose two children; and they know about it. They will be the ones who research your illness to become more familiar with it because someone they love is suffering. They will be the ones who show up every night to help you with your injection treatment and never once complain. They will be the ones who check in on you in the middle of a Wednesday afternoon just to see how you are holding up. They will be the ones who send you a card just to let you know they are thinking of you. They will be the ones who get on a plane in the blink of an eye when you lose your first child because they know that seeing their face will brighten your world. They will be the ones who make you feel known and understood.

When you take a step back, the large number of people that you love will not be a part of your "inner circle." I have a ton of people in my life that I would do anything for, who I love unconditionally and accept them for who they are. But the truth is there are only a few people of that large population that I would call if I truly needed a listening ear. The other people matter to me; don't get me wrong, I would be lost without all them, and my life would not be the same. But just because you love someone, and they love you back does not mean they have earned the right to get to know your deepest and darkest stories. Some people live in their own bubble and only peek through when it benefits them.

Even though, for your own sanity, you cannot share every piece of your world with everyone in it, this does not negate the fact that some of those people play a large role in your life inspirations. Inspiration can flow from many different angles. Some people who inspire you are at the center of your circle, while other inspirations come from people who bring you the most frustration. I am going to share with you the stories of the people that have personally inspired me to be who I am today. Most of these people are a part of my circle; however, there are two unique inspirations that I want to share with you first. These two people fall into a category of their own. This is the category that I like to describe as "temporary interactions with permanent impact." I think this is my favorite type of connection made with people. An example of this type of connection would be the person you pass on the street that leaves a lasting image imbedded in your brain.

Someone whose name you do not know, who you most likely will never see again, but who tugs on your heartstrings harder than people you have known your whole life. In my own personal story, the two people are a college professor that I knew for five months and a woman that I met on a plane and spoke to for two hours.

Throughout my years in school, I was blessed to have educators who impacted my life in many ways. I have many memories of lessons taught to me, but one stood out among the rest. The year was 2011, and I was taking a large variety of college courses. However, this interaction happened in the hallway of the Business Building and not in the classroom. I was walking home to my dorm after wrapping up class, and I happened to pass by another professor near the coffee shop. We made eye contact, and I gave him one of those Midwestern passerby smiles accompanied with a small head nod to nonverbally say "hello." Just before he was about to pass me by on my left-hand side, I broke eye contact and dropped my head down toward the ground and kept walking. Over my shoulder I heard a deep voice say, "Never again." Confused, I kept walking. I then heard the same voice say, "Hey, Melissa, I was talking to you, and I said *never again!*"

Being the Goody Two-shoes that I am, I immediately began to panic. "What could I have possibly done?" I thought to myself. Feeling worried that I offended him somehow, I turned around and asked him what I did and immediately began to apologize, despite having no idea what I was apologizing for. He asked me if I had a few moments to spare and if so, to grab a seat with him at the coffee shop. I had no plans and was thoroughly intrigued as to what this was all about, so I grabbed a seat and let him explain.

He went on to tell me that he thought I was one of the most confident students he had in class, but what just happened in our short interaction contradicted his thoughts of me. He said that the moment I broke eye contact and put my head down before passing him displayed weakness. He asked me why I did it. I explained to him that when I hold eye contact in passing it feels like time slows down, and it becomes awkward, so I am used to making it short and sweet and then looking away. It is how I have always done it since I could remember.

What he told me next is the piece that has stuck with me to this date and will stick with me forever. He went on to explain that since I want to go into the business world, the harsh reality is that most large corporations are run by men. These men would almost always be older than me and would most likely be stuck in an old school frame of mind. He said that weakness does not allow people to advance as far as they should in the real world, and looking down at the ground when walking past someone is a display of weakness. He was not saying it in a way to hurt me or to call me weak. He was saying it in a kind and caring way as to look out for me and help me grow as a person. He left that conversation after telling me that there was no reason to look away. There was no reason to drop my head. He told me to walk tall and hold my head up high, and I would be surprised how much more seriously people would take me if I looked them in the eye and walked proud.

You might not think much of it and consider it not that big of a deal, but ever since that conversation that I had with him years ago, I make it a point to try to not break eye contact when passing by someone. I am not perfect, and sometimes it still feels awkward, and I want to lower my eyes and head. However, every time that thought comes into my mind, I go back to the coffee shop in 2011 where I was taught an extremely valuable life lesson. That day, my professor took time out of his day, out of his classroom, to teach me something about myself that I needed to hear. Also, he was right; I have worked with many men in my years thus far who are older and higher up than I am. However, I do not feel intimidated by their titles. That does not mean I do not respect them. In fact, I have the utmost respect for what they do. What it does mean, though, is that just because they wear a suit and make quadruple my salary, it does not negate the fact that they are human. When I pass them in the hallway at work, I stop to ask them how they are doing or make small talk. Not to try to stand out more, but to let it be known that my gender and rank in the company does not make me any less of a person than they are. My confidence level drastically changed in 2011, and I owe that inspiration to a man who took ten minutes to teach me something I would have never learned by sitting in the classroom.

My encounter with my professor was the second time in my life that I was presented with a temporary interaction that would have a permanent impact. The first time occurred five years prior in 2006 on a flight from Chicago to New York. My mom and I had a trip planned to go visit family together. Unfortunately, it came after a very hard time for me and my family. Without going into too much detail to share about his story, my dad was given a diagnosis a few months prior that left me feeling very confused. (Spoiler alert: he is doing incredible these days. More about that later!). Back to the trip, I was experiencing all sorts of emotions daily at that time. It was the first time I would be seeing all my extended family in a while, and I just really was not looking forward to talking about sadness all day and night.

We boarded the plane. I was in the aisle seat, my mom was in the middle, and a stranger was against the window. My mom and I are talkers, so it did not take long after takeoff for us to strike up a conversation with the lady next to us. Within the first few seconds, we could hear that there was a bit of a slur in her words, and at times it was difficult to understand her. We did not discuss too much to begin with, but then it was lunchtime. I will never forget the white bag that she had her salad in, which was tucked under the seat in front of her. She leaned forward, grabbed the bag with her right hand, and brought it up on the tray. The nosey people that we both are, my mom and I looked over and noticed that she was trying to open the plastic bag while only using her right hand. My mom offered to help her, and she humbly agreed. My mom took the salad out of the bag, took the lid off it, put the dressing on for her, and made sure she was good to go. We would never be the ones to initiate asking her anything about what was wrong, but deep down we were curious.

The woman began to open up to us about how she was heading to New York for a layover before flying home to Texas. She said that the last few years had been hard on her ever since she had a stroke and lost the function in her left arm. I wish more than anything I could have recorded that conversation because so young, I only remember bits and pieces. She spoke about how she had to move in with her son because the tasks that once came easy for her slowly became more challenging. Despite admitting that she needed assistance from time to time, she was in the best spirits. I remember her talking in a way full of gratitude. She sounded thankful for every moment, was grateful for the little things, and showed a sense of humility that was evident even to someone my age. She had absolutely no idea the struggles my family was facing in these times and how her words meant more to me than she could imagine. The next words she said had a permanent impact on me. She looked at me and confidently said, "fight, fight." She went on to explain that no matter what battle you are faced with in life, and when the world tries to knock you down, the only thing you can do is hold your head high and "Fight, fight." There is not much more I remember after those words because I silently sat there with tears rolling down my face and trying not to full on lose it on an airplane. Everything she was saying was the hope I needed in that time of my life; it in fact brought me hope far beyond that moment.

Her words did not only have a permanent impact on my heart, but literally have had a permanent impact on my body. When I turned eighteen, I got a tattoo that represented the battle my dad had been faced with. Inside of the tattoo, I had the words "fight, fight" embedded. There was not a more perfect saying that I could think of that I wanted to keep with me forever. I have lost count of the number of times I have said those words over the years. I have memories of presurgery when I would hug and kiss my mom, and she would look at me, smile, grab my hand, and declare, "fight, fight." Whenever the going would get rough—and as you have seen thus far in my story, the rough happened often—I would constantly reiterate the words "fight, fight" to myself to try and push through. I will never know the name of the woman next to the window on the airplane that day; I will never know how she is doing today, and she will never know the permanent impact that our temporary interaction has had on me. It was a beautiful moment that inspired me beyond belief.

Between the amount of confidence and hope that I gained over those interactions, I felt like a changed person as I grew older. I have flashbacks of those two moments from 2006 and 2011 all the time whenever I feel defeated or weak. They are my examples of people who impacted my life and inspired me but are not a part of my "inner circle." There is a whole other group of people that I want to introduce you to. Some are family, and some are friends, but all of them inspire me and have shaped me into the person I am today.

First and foremost, I must pay tribute to the one who is at the center of my life—Jesus Christ. I did not grow up always knowing who Jesus was. It was not until I was ten years old that I ever really heard stories about Him. You see, I grew up Jewish, but I never felt connected to the religion. The best way I can describe it is that my parents, brother, and I were only Jewish when it came to holidays and food. Being Jewish for us meant that on certain days throughout the year, we would cook traditional meals and partake in some activities. However, every other day of the year there was no connection to the religion. Shortly after my parents got divorced, my dad was invited to attend a nondenominational church service, and he loved the feeling of what being a Christian truly meant. We were with my dad on Sundays, so it was not long before my brother and I started to attend the services with him. I remember everyone being so kind and full of this overwhelming sense of peace and happiness. I always looked forward to going each week. A few months down the road, my mom was invited to a wedding that was held at a different nondenominational church near our hometown. It didn't take her long to begin attending church as well on a regular basis. So, at that point, regardless of which parent we were spending time with, Jesus, church, and the Bible were regular conversations that filled our homes. I quickly learned through each of them leading me that Christianity was not just a religion; it was about a deep relationship with Jesus Christ—believing that He is the son of God and that He died to take away the sins of the world. My parents each got baptized, and I witnessed the change in each of them for the better.

When I was twelve, I made the decision to get baptized and to publicly declare my love for Jesus Christ. It was one of the most memorable days of my life. Jesus is not just a part of my life on Sundays or on holidays when families traditionally gather for a meal. He is at the center of everything I do day in and day out, and I could not be prouder of my relationship that I have developed with Him. I have clearly been faced with many dark times throughout my infertility journey, but never once did my faith waver. I do not blame God for one piece of it. If anything, I am oddly grateful for the hard times that I faced. Obviously, I am not grateful for losing two children and suffering so much pain, but I am grateful that each hurdle only brought me closer in my relationship to Jesus. He suffered on the cross, and if He could do that, I can do anything. I truly believe that if it was not for the devastating situations that I have been faced with, I would not be where I am at today in my faith journey. Sometimes it takes hitting an all-time low before you can stand tall, look yourself in the eye, and see how far you have truly come. I personally owe that strength to Jesus. All the glory goes to Him.

The next person who is a part of my "inner circle" is my husband, Chris. I have been struggling with how to write about him, not because I do not know what to say, but because everything I come up with does not seem to do him justice. This man is an absolute angel on earth. We met in college and remained friends for two years postgraduation until one day in 2014 he took me on a date … that I did not even know was a date. We connected for years through sports, especially baseball. In May 2014, the Yankees were set to play the Brewers in Milwaukee, and we had plans to catch the game together. However, I was so sick I was not able to go. Instead, he drove from Wisconsin to Illinois to watch the game with me on television. We had wings, and he brought me cookie dough ice cream, Big League Chew, a Milwaukee Brewers stuffed animal dog, and a jersey so that it was like we were at the game together while in my living room. After the game, he drove back home, and I thought nothing of it. I was so naive that someone I knew for so many years would have wanted to be more than friends with me. On my birthday a couple of weeks later, he kissed me, and then it all made sense. However, I still stand firm to this day that the baseball date was not really a date because there must be an unwritten rule somewhere that both parties involved must be made aware when a date is occurring.

One of us—me—had absolutely no idea it was a date, so it does not count. We agree to disagree on this.

The last thing I ever wanted to do was to risk ruining one of the best friendships I had at that time in my life, but two years later we got married, and it was the best decision I have ever made. Not only did I not lose a friend, but I gained a husband who remains the strongest friendship and relationship in my life. Every single day is a blessing that I get to spend time with him, laugh, and be in the presence of someone who makes me a better person. I dated a few people before him, and none of those men knew how to handle me at my worst when I would have endometriosis attacks. It scared me that no one would be able to understand what I needed in a life partner to see me through the struggles. Chris never failed me—not once. Neither one of us knew that the infertility piece would be a part of our story when we decided to get married. A lot of men would run or lose compassion along the way, but not him. He is my rock, and I could not imagine having to go through the tragedies I have faced with anyone by my side but him.

Countless times over the years, I would awake in the middle of the night scared, in pain, or crying over fear, and he would wake up with me every single time. Sometimes to just hold me, others to do research for me, and at times to simply rub my back and reassure me that everything was going to be okay because we were in it together; whatever that "it" might have been at the time. I lost count of how many shots for treatment I needed at home, but it reached somewhere in the hundreds over the years. This man never missed a shot, leaving me to do it alone. No matter what his work schedule looked like or if friends asked him to do something at night, he was home around seven o'clock every single night to give me an injection. I have a dresser full of medicine and needles in our spare room where we would meet every night. On that dresser are some motivational knickknacks that I used to pump myself up before each shot. As time went on, the chant got longer with more positive sayings involved. However, the original saying that would get me ready for a shot came directly from Chris. He would look me in the eyes every night and say, "Now remember, I love you very much, and I do not mean to hurt you, but now I have to hurt you. You're just going to feel a little pinch. And I love you very much. Okay, 3-2-1." As the needle went in and the medicine would begin to get injected, the pain started rising. I would, by instinct, begin to hold my breath. Then I would hear, "I don't hear you breathing, give me some big breaths … good job … and … we're done!" His gentle soul that is full of compassion and patience is my favorite thing about him. The mountains we have climbed together over the years are higher than some people face in a lifetime, but the keyword here is, together. Together, there is nothing that we cannot accomplish.

The next person I want to share with everyone is someone you have read about a few times up to this point. She is my mom, Karen, a.k.a., my person. Growing up, I can count on one hand the number of big disagreements or arguments we had. There has always been this unspoken natural connection where we understand each other on a deeper level. She can know how I am feeling without me saying a word and vice versa. She did not have it the easiest when she was younger, and most would agree did not have the best example of what a supportive mom looked like; yet somehow she became someone who embodies the true definition of what unconditional love is. There was no mistake I made over the years where she made me feel less than or unworthy. There is not a single example that I can think of where she used words to cut me down or belittle me—even if she disagreed with a choice of mine. One of the best life lessons she taught me is that money does not make someone happy. A house is just a house unless you are under the roof with people you cannot survive without; that is what made her house a home. Home was always wherever she was. One of my favorite memories growing up was when we would stop everything for a few moments just to dance in the kitchen. No music and definitely no professional moves. Just two people letting loose and laughing. It does not get better than that.

When my endometriosis journey began, she showed up to every single appointment and listened attentively to better understand my situation. I felt abandoned by many people in my life emotionally when the pain was unbearable, but never once did I feel this from my mom. To put into words how thankful I am for this incredible woman in my life is impossible; no words do her justice. She is my go-to in all things, the one I can share anything with and never feel judged, and the one who I look up to. There really is no greater reward than having a parent who doubles as your best friend as you grow up. Life is short and unpredictable, and I am so glad I have a relationship with my mom that allows me to constantly make incredible memories that I can carry with me forever.

While my mom has played, and continues to play, a pivotal

role in my life, I would be remiss not to mention my dad. Next to the word *perseverance* in the dictionary should be a picture of my dad. When it comes to perseverance, there is no one in my life who embodies this word better. I hinted a bit earlier in the book about a health struggle that my dad was faced with and how he has continued to overcome all obstacles over the years surrounding it. With respect as to not share his journey through my words, the very basic version is that he was diagnosed with a brain tumor in early 2006. There were a few bumps in the road around 2012 where some treatment was needed, but aside from that rough patch, he has always chosen the homeopathic, faith-based route without the aid of medication that destroys the body. His attitude surrounding this diagnosis never once caused his faith in God to waiver. It has been beyond admirable to watch someone get news that normally would cause a person to crumble, but in his case, he stood tall and did not let it shake him one bit.

My dad was always a present father growing up. My family jokes that there must have been something in the water around the time of my parent's divorce because it seemed like everyone was doing it. I had so many classmates whose parents divorced around the same time, and most of their dads moved hours away, out of state, and some even out of the country. My parents lived fifteen minutes apart, and both showed up to every single sporting event and milestone in my life. Being able to look into the stands and see both parents sitting and cheering me on is something I took for granted back then but as an adult appreciate more than they will ever know.

We definitely did not always see eye to eye over the years. In fact, there were a lot of times I did not feel close to my dad. I know that he loves and adores me and that has never been something I have ever had to question, but I would be lying if I said I always felt that emotional support from him. Part of the reason, if not most of it, is due to my fear. My dad and I had screaming matches like you would not believe when I was growing up, and I had it ingrained in my brain that the loudest person during a fight was the one who was winning. As I grew older, I realized how unhealthy that was. There were times where my fear of a simple conversation turning into a fight caused me to not open up to my dad, and that has not always been fair to him. I had, and often still have, a presumed assumption of a response that he will give to a scenario in my head that will keep me from being completely honest with him. If I would get out of my head at times, he and I could have a rock-solid relationship. Do not get me wrong; he is incredible, and I do feel close to him, just probably not as close as we could be if I let go of past hurt. I am hoping to work on that soon to be able to build the relationship I have always desired to have with him. Nonetheless, I know without a doubt in my mind that he is so proud of all I have endured physically, mentally, and emotionally throughout my infertility battle. I learned along the way to persevere through anything life throws at me, just like my dad has always done.

If you think back to when I discussed the surprise visit that I received in 2019 postsurgery for my birthday, you will remember the next person that I want to discuss—my little brother, Brandon. Brandon and I are four years apart. Growing up with him was amazing. I learned to appreciate our relationship at a very young age. When my parents got divorced, I was nine, and Brandon was five. Who would have thought I would be so dependent on a five-year-old? No matter which house we were at during specific days of the week, we were always together. Of course, there were plenty of times where his little brother annoyances would kick in, but I wouldn't have it any other way if it all were to happen again. He was my constant throughout the years. If there were times of uncertainty that would leave me anxious, I knew he would be right there next to me, and it made me feel at peace. As we grew older, we chose different paths in life in many ways, but I always remained hopeful and proud of him. I watched as he hit what I would consider to be rock bottom on a few occasions, and it would break my heart each time. But he knew I would always be there with a shoulder to cry on and with an ear to listen. There were a few years around the time that I went away to college where I felt like our relationship faded, but postgraduation, we picked up right where we left off, if not stronger. Shortly after Chris and I got engaged, Brandon decided to live out a dream and move out west to California. I was living in Illinois at the time of his move, and now I got a taste of what it was like to live near our hometown with a puzzle piece missing. I selfishly longed for him to move back, and luckily, he did just that after a couple of months.

After my grandma passed away in 2018, he decided to live life to the fullest and not take a single moment for granted. He took the opportunity to live out another dream and picked up to move to Arizona. This time, however, it was different. This time he was not making the venture to another state alone; he had his other half with him. As much as I was going to miss him being so far away yet again, there was nothing but happiness that filled my heart in knowing he had someone to share his life with and start fresh. Kegan and Brandon are getting married in 2021, and I could not be happier with who he chose to spend forever with. The way that they both have supported Chris and me through all the ups and downs has been one of the biggest blessings in our lives. They are both the type of people who listen attentively and truly care. They remember important dates and send words of encouragement to help us continue to push through. There are times I wish I could blink my eyes, and we would be nine and five again and go back to all the incredible memories of growing up together, but knowing I have a brother for a best friend as an adult is something I would never trade in. His perspective on life, respectfulness of others, and compassionate heart are just a few reasons why my brother is one of my biggest inspirations in life.

There are two other parents that I have in my life aside from my mom and dad; they are my stepmom, Michelle, and my stepdad, Jeff. There is no written rule that says all parents must love their children, and there definitely is not a rule that says stepparents must love their stepchildren. Lucky for me, I was blessed with two people who entered my life by choice and chose to love me like their own. Through the marriage of my dad to Michelle, I gained a stepbrother and stepsister. It did not take us siblings long to drop the "step." It would get confusing early on trying to explain how many brothers and sisters I had if someone were to ask, so naturally it just became two brothers and one sister. My mom married Jeff, or as I like to call him my D2, in 2011. He also had a son and daughter from a previous marriage. So, our little family of four clearly became a bit more like something you would see on a comedy television show. The amount of love that is poured out through my family—the one that is chosen and not through blood—runs endlessly. The support that I am shown from my stepparents and bonus siblings is something that I will not ever take for granted. It might not be your fairy tale family story, but it is mine, and I would not trade it for the world.

Real and authentic friendships are especially hard to come by as you get older; they seemed much easier when you were a kid. For me, I am blessed with a lot of really good friends, but none that compare to my friend Melanie. Melanie and I met shortly after I started my first big girl job in 2013. In November of that year, there was a volunteer opportunity through work with special needs children at a local elementary school. I went that day not knowing anyone and had an experience I will never forget as I watched those little eyes light up while at a carnival in their gym. It was rewarding to be surrounded by so much joy in such a short amount of time. While there, I started a conversation with a girl around my age with big curly hair just like me. I remembered her first name but could not remember her last. I found her that next week on our company's internal chatting system. (In other words, I stalked our site until I came across her name. Yes, creepy I know, but it was worth it). We worked in different departments and quickly became friends. At this time, we were each living at home with about a forty-minute commute one way to the office and really wanted to move closer, but it was so expensive. So, we came up with the idea to become roommates the next summer and split the costs. It was one of the best decisions I ever made.

Not only did the commute go from forty minutes to five minutes, but I gained a lifelong friend.

Melanie is a one-of-a-kind human being. I have never met anyone else with such a solid heart of gold. She is the type of friend that makes you want to become a better person. Every single thing she puts her mind to, she gives 110 percent. The proof is in her homemade cards. This girl gives the best cards full of stickers, quotes, and thought beyond anything I have ever gifted anyone with. She is the type of friend you can talk to about everything. We chat about family, music, movies, goals, struggles, achievements, fears, and best of all, it is always a no judgment zone. It is an effortless friendship like they all should be. If we do not see each other for an extended amount of time, there is no blame. We both understand that life is busy, but no matter what we always will make the best of the time we do get to spend together. When I went through the losses of Raspberry and Cranberry, gifts were sitting on my front porch each time with the intent to cheer me up and to be reminded that through the loneliness I was in fact not alone. My wish for everyone is to find that one solid friendship and never let it go.

The last piece of my "inner circle" is not just one person, but rather a group of people. In January 2019, one week after I was starting my IVF treatment, I logged into my work computer and in the center of our welcome screen was an advertisement that the company was starting an Infertility and Loss Support Group right there at the corporate building. I could not believe what my eyes were seeing; the timing could not have been any more perfect. However, my initial reaction was that there was no way

I was about to join that group. Why would I want the people I work under the same roof with to know my deepest and darkest secrets? That thought lasted about ten minutes until I decided it could not hurt to at least sign up for email notifications for when the meetings would be, and then at that point I could choose to attend or not. I spoke to Chris and my mom about it, and after the discussions I decided to take the leap of faith and go. A week or so later, I attended my first meeting; and boy was I glad I went.

This group of incredibly strong women showed me that I am not alone in my pain and that there are others out in the world just like me. We all have different stories and struggles, but the commonality is that we all understand the level of compassion it takes to support someone through the devastation. We meet once a month, and it is such a great stress reliever. It is like free therapy with women who have become friends and empathize with where I am coming from. I am forever grateful to my company for starting up this group. Deciding to not hide in fear and shame and attending my first meeting is something I am so proud of myself for doing. If I had not, I would have never had this group of women in my corner during every high and every low.

Everyone that you read about, from Jesus to my support group, make up what I have been calling my "inner circle." They are the people who make me better and have my back in ways no one else can. There are still other people in my life that I would not be the same without, but those relationships are on a different level than the ones above. I have incredible grandparents who never fail to tell me how much they love me, friends from high school and college that add so much joy to my life, family

I've gained through marriage, friends who really became more like chosen family years ago who have changed my world for the better, and so many more loved ones who I am so thankful for that words do not do them justice. The point I am trying to make is that not every single person you cross paths with in life from birth to death needs to know every piece of your whole life. There are some that belong in your circle because there is a mutual respect and understanding that fits into your life differently than other relationships. It does not make the relationships outside of that circle any less important than the ones inside; they are just different. The root of where most of my inspiration comes from is directly from the people that I have chosen to walk this crazy journey of life with. Next, I will share with you the faithful fight that ultimately strengthened me.

5

The Faithful Fight That Strengthened Me

A few years back, I shared a dream with someone and that person's response was, "You went to business school; you are meant to sit behind a desk, so just do that." It does not really matter what that dream was at the time, and in all honesty, it probably was too far-fetched for the work I was willing to dedicate to it, but the response stuck with me throughout the years. I did in fact go to business school, but I never felt like my entire life's purpose was to be fulfilled behind a desk. I am more than my nine to five and more than my degree. I have stories to tell and people that I want to inspire, and there is no reason I cannot do it all. I was asked by someone in recent years what I want my purpose in life to be and to come up with a purpose statement. This was all amid the treatment I was going through, but for whatever reason I never linked up my infertility story to my purpose statement. When I wrote my purpose statement, I was thinking of another dream I had in mind, which was to eventually learn sign language. With that being the picture I was focused on, the purpose statement that I wrote was, "My purpose is to bring people together in order to bridge the gap of presumed indifferences."

As time progressed, life got busy, and I did not end up dedicating as much time to learning sign language as I had originally hoped to do. I felt like my purpose statement failed due to not pursuing this dream as strongly as I wanted to. But then, I had a realization within this last year. Maybe I came up with this statement through a subconscious thought of infertility at the center and not sign language. I realized I could shift the intention behind this purpose to bring people together to bridge the gap of presumed indifferences as it relates to any invisible illness. It is easy for everyone with a disease to think that they are alone, but once we start talking about our pain, we realize we are not all that different. My hope and prayer has always been to bring awareness to these issues to make at least one person feel seen, known, and understood. Therefore, I no longer believe that my purpose failed. In fact, I feel like after all the struggles, I have begun to achieve my purpose. That does not mean I am finished, as there is a lot more work to be done. But at the end of the day, I can successfully look back and know that for all the lost dreams, I did not lose when it came to this one.

There is one more piece to my incredibly complex puzzle that must be shared. Toward the end of the chapter centered on my treatment, I mentioned that there was a third and final embryo transfer that we were preparing for. Fear not, I did not forget to close the gap on this crucially important part of the journey. The testing was complete, and we were cleared for our transfer date on March 24, 2020. To say I was nervous beyond belief does not begin to scratch the surface of my feelings surrounding that day. To know that if this failed, we would never have a biological child was something my brain could not comprehend. But just as I had done in the past, I walked into the doctor's office that day with my head held high, took a deep breath (more like twenty deep breaths), and proceeded with the transfer. Now, the dreadful ten-day waiting period began before the blood draw to confirm HCG levels. The day before, I cheated and took a test. Ten days to wait was too long; nine sounded nicer. It was positive, and I was so excited, but in the back of my mind, there was still so much fear about what the blood draw the next day would show and if this was going to be just like my previous situations; positive to start off with but then a decrease in numbers and more bad news to come.

My first HCG value ended up coming back at 248. To give you some perspective, with our first baby, the first draw came back at sixty-three and with the second pregnancy the first draw came back at thirteen. So, with a number this high compared to my other two experiences, hope grew. Three days later, another draw needed to be done to make sure that the number more than doubled. They really do not care what the first number is if the second number is significantly higher. The rule of thumb tends to be that the number result needs to double every forty-eight hours. The phone rang, and I rambled to the nurse that my history was never good with this second phone call. I was so nervous for whatever she was about to say and asked her to be gentle with it because I felt like my heart was going to explode. That is when she said the words, "I have nothing but great news for you. Your second draw HCG level is 1,038. You are really pregnant!" I lost it. I am talking full-blown hysterics. I kept screaming the number back to her and yelling, "Thank you!" This news called for a dance party with no music (much like the one my mom and I used to have growing up) and a lot of jumping around. Picture Rocky climbing the stairs with both fists pumping in the air; that was me but living room style.

Getting to share the news with immediate family came with a mix of emotions. Everyone was extremely happy and that was when my anxiety started to rise. I knew that despite the positive numbers coming back, we were not out of the woods yet. There were still the obligatory appointments to confirm the baby was growing exactly where it needed to be. We'd already experienced the opposite of that once before. I still needed to receive shots every day for many more weeks. The last thing I ever wanted to do was to create this high for everyone just to shatter all their hopes and dreams yet again for a third time. I knew that as excited as I was for this miraculous news, in the back of my mind, I could not stop the negative thoughts from creeping in no matter how hard I tried to push them out.

My infertility doctor wanted to see me for what she called a placement ultrasound. Although the baby at this point would be near impossible to see except by a trained eye, she wanted to confirm that the baby was growing in my uterus. Due to the global pandemic of Covid-19 being in full swing at this point, Chris was not allowed to come into the ultrasound with me. Luckily, she allowed me to video chat with him during the appointment, but it was not how I imagined this piece of the puzzle looking. On April 9, 2020, I went to the clinic, prayed, and took a seat on that uncomfortable paper that was draped on top of the examination table. Here went nothing. The monitor reflected what looked to me like a bunch of black and white lines and circles. I had no idea what I was looking at. However, with one small move of the ultrasound wand, there it was—the most perfect little dot I have ever seen. The doctor confirmed that the little dot was indeed our baby, and it was exactly where it was supposed to be; tucked perfectly inside of my uterus. A huge milestone had been accomplished, and it felt incredible to be able to walk out of the office that day with happy tears instead of distraught ones.

Just as with my previous processes, there has always been a waiting game after each accomplishment. This time was no different. My doctor wanted me to wait two weeks and then come back to see her to detect a heartbeat. The crazy part about this step would be that if everything checked out positively, I would be officially discharged from the infertility clinic. That whole picture in my head seemed so surreal because I did not even remember what life looked like without being under their care. April 23, 2020, approached in what both felt like a lifetime and in the blink of an eye. Like before, Chris was not able to join me inside for the appointment, but he was able to join through a video call again. This appointment was full of so many emotions. I went into it assuming we would get to hear the heartbeat, but when the doctor came into the room, she explained that listening to the heartbeat that early in pregnancy could cause problems to the baby. So, instead, she was going to measure the beats per minute without any noise.

Understandably, I was immediately disappointed because I'd set my expectation for this appointment so high to finally be able to hear the baby's heartbeat. On the contrary, the moment that I saw the flicker on the screen, all disappointment disappeared. Watching my baby's heart beating from inside of me is a feeling I will never forget. Our determined baby had a strong heartbeat of 157 beats per minute. With that news came another wave of emotions. Now that all the boxes were checked, I was an official graduate from the infertility clinic. My doctor and team of nurses who held my hand through every trial, tribulation, and celebratory moment, and who made me feel so known and understood with every step of the journey, had played such a large role in my life. Knowing I would not be seeing them anymore crushed a piece of me. The support I felt from them was like nothing I'd ever known from the staff at an office building before. My last emotion was how truly proud of myself I felt. I told myself at the beginning of the journey that I would see everything through to the end and never give up. Believe me, there were many times I wanted to, but I held on and kept going. To know that the third time was the charm, and if I had given up, I would not have a healthy baby growing just proves that it was all worth it. Granted, the battle was not over quite yet, but graduating from this step in the journey was a huge accomplishment, and the only way I can describe it is that I was so genuinely proud of myself.

Through a referral from my infertility doctor, I was able to find an OBGYN who specialized in endometriosis and was within the same hospital network. This made the transfer to my new doctor extremely easy because medical records were within their system, and I did not need to work on gathering years' worth of papers to bring to my initial appointment. If you have ever needed to transfer doctors outside of your original network, you know the pain I am referring to here. My first appointment with my new doctor was on April 28, 2020. Despite COVID-19 still being very real and present, this office allowed one visitor into the room with the patient. That meant that Chris would be able to join me. Our doctor felt comfortable playing the noise on the ultrasound while measuring the baby's heartbeat, so together for the very first time, we got to hear the beautiful beats of our baby's perfect heart. This time the beats per minute measured at a whopping 163. If nothing else, we had a very strong baby growing at this point. We also got to see the baby's cute little arms starting to form; an image I will never get out of my mind. This day was full of so many blessings.

Our baby proved to be exactly like its momma in the next week—punctual to the minute. I was told that at seven weeks nausea and morning sickness would most likely kick in. If you are doing the math at this point you might be thinking I am three weeks ahead of schedule, and there is no way I was already seven weeks along. However, something that we learned was that a frozen embryo transfer is calculated differently than a normal pregnancy. A few weeks get added on to the beginning without me having the baby implanted during that time. Crazy, right? Anyway, back to the punctuality of my unborn child. The moment seven weeks struck the clock, the nausea hit like no other. Constant sickness is the only way to describe it. Whoever came up with the term morning sickness got it really wrong. All day sickness is a much better way to describe my situation. At one point between weeks seven and ten, I was so sick that I was terrified I was dehydrated. To play it safe, we went to urgent care.

Luckily, I was low on the spectrum of what they consider to be dehydrated since I was able to at least keep some water down during these days. I started going to sleep around five o'clock most nights just because if I was sleeping, then at least I was not curled up on the bathroom floor hugging the toilet. My weight kept dropping. I went from 129 pounds from my transfer date in March to 117 pounds the first week of May. It became depressing at times because all I wanted was to be able to feel healthy and ensure that my baby was safe, and at this point I was so far from feeling that.

The ten-week mark hit, and it was time for another huge milestone—my last progesterone shot ever. Due to the baby being implanted via IVF, the levels of my progesterone were not being created as the body normally would do if you get pregnant the natural way. Because of this, I needed to continue my progesterone shots until I hit ten weeks of pregnancy. On May 14, 2020, I hit the day that I had been looking forward to for so long. It was a very bittersweet day for me, but not for the reason you might think. This date marked two years from when my grandma unexpectedly passed away. It blew my mind that two full years had already come and gone without her being around to share any of my rollercoaster with. I spent most of the day reflecting on how much I missed her and how incredibly proud she would have been to know I was carrying her great-grandchild. At seven o'clock that night, just as I had every night, I prepped for my injection in my makeshift hospital room—a.k.a. the spare bedroom. The difference this time was that my mom, stepdad, brother, and soon to be sister-in-law all video called in so they could join in on the celebration of my very last injection. To know I had all this love and support around me contributed to this day of emotions. Chris injected me with my very last shot ever, and my family cheered. I started to cry because I could not believe this other milestone had now been accomplished. At this point, I had three medical waste bins full of hundreds of used needles in the drawer in the dresser of the room. When seven o'clock hit the next evening, it felt like a piece of me was missing. This nightly ritual had been going on for so long at this point that I thought I was forgetting something. As the nights passed, it became more normal to not need to prep for a shot, but it took a while to get used to.

Somehow, I blinked, and we were already at the twelve-week mark, which meant it was time for another check-up with the doctor. The baby was so incredibly active during the scan. It kept dancing around, kicking its feet, and pumping its arm up and down. Chris likes to describe this situation as, "the baby was twerking the whole time!" It was so rewarding to get to see the growth, especially because I could not feel a single movement. It all felt surreal. The doctor confirmed the baby's heart was very strong and was beating at 159 beats per minute. This week also consisted of another milestone but not so much baby related. I turned the big 3-0 within week twelve of pregnancy.

My original dream had always been to tour the Greek islands for my golden, thirtieth birthday. I imagined touring around Athens, sailing to Mykonos, and admiring the beauty of Santorini since I could remember. I spent years doing research surrounding the exact places I needed to see and had this huge dream that I was ready to accomplish, until I realized how expensive it would end up being. The reality was that to do everything I wanted to do, it would take roughly fourteen days of a getaway versus our normal weeklong time frame that we would set aside per adventure. So as time got closer, I became more realistic and decided it was wiser to wait a few years to take this dream trip. In the end that worked out well, because on top of the above hurdles, there was this little (not so little) worldwide virus of Covid-19 happening smack-dab in the middle of my birthday, which meant we would not have been able to travel even if we wanted to. Oh yeah, and also, I was pregnant. I am glad I did not invest actual dollars into this dream because, clearly, I was not meant to accomplish it in the year 2020. The backup plan was going to be to have a party with all my friends and family that my gracious husband was going to put together. But due to regulations of gathering size from the virus, this plan also ended up being botched. So, instead, I turned thirty by eating pizza, fruit, and cake while in a social distant circle with eight immediate family members in our backyard. Probably not comparable to the time I would have had in Greece or partying with everyone in my life, but the baby absolutely loved every bite of food that day, so in the end, I would consider it a great and memorable celebration.

Everyone says that the time goes by exceptionally fast when you are expecting. At first, I felt the complete opposite. The first trimester felt like it was never going to end, which could have been due in large part to the overwhelming amount of sickness I was experiencing day in and day out. However, once the second trimester was in full swing, looking back, the time definitely did fly by. I was told by multiple people, including my own doctor, that everything should subside around the fourteenth week. My baby, being the overachiever that it clearly was, wanted to prove everyone wrong and stretch out the sickness for many more weeks. It was not until roughly the end of week seventeen that I was finally able to feel human again and digest more than dry foods and water.

There were so many milestones that the baby was rapidly accomplishing throughout these first few weeks of the second trimester. Vocal cords began forming, facial muscles allowed for smiles, sense of hearing continued to strengthen, and lungs started to develop. If my sickness had to be prolonged just a little while longer to grow this healthy, strong baby, then every trip to the bathroom was worth it. During week sixteen, we had a doctor's appointment for a check-up. Our doctor only allowed us to do the Doppler this time, and we were not able to see the baby during this appointment. I had become fixated on paying attention to the doctor during appointments at this point to see if their facial expressions would indicate something was wrong. At this appointment, the doctor was trying to find the baby's heartbeat and the noise I heard coming from the Doppler sounded like a water motion and not a heart pounding. I was staring at the doctor's face as she moved the device around on my stomach, and I got instantly nervous. This all lasted about thirty seconds, but in the moment, it felt much longer. Suddenly, she pulled back and said, "Everything is perfect. The baby's heart rate is in the low 150 beats per minute." To which I replied, "Oh, that noise was the heart?" Who knew! Her face was not one of concern but rather that of concentration. Even if during this appointment we could not see the baby, the reassurance of having a healthy growing human inside of me made everything okay.

It was now time for baby's first adventure. We originally had a trip to Utah planned for a weeklong getaway, but due to the pandemic, flying did not sound like the most enjoyable (or wisest) option out there. We moved our trip to Branson, Missouri, so that we could drive instead of fly. It was by no means a close second to what our experience in Utah would have been like, but it did allow us to get out of the house for a few days and decompress from the craziness that consumed our lives over the past four months. With stopping to eat and stretch, the drive took about eleven hours, and overall, the baby did so well in the sense of making me feel comfortable. Throughout the week, the baby tried new foods, went on its first hike, went swimming for the first time, and was super active during the music shows we saw at night. We hit a few bumps in the road with sickness toward the back end of the trip and had one emergency need to pull over on the side of the road on the way home, to not destroy the rental car. But nonetheless, I was so proud of the baby for its cooperation in allowing me to enjoy the trip and sneak in some relaxation. And I cannot forget about the most exciting part of all. Chris happened to have his hand on my stomach to say hi to the baby on July 8, and suddenly the baby moved with such might and strength. He was so happy, with the biggest smile on his face, when he got to feel the baby move for the first time.

The long-awaited day of July 24, 2020, had finally arrived. At a whopping twenty weeks and one day along in the pregnancy, it was time for our anatomy scan. We had been anticipating this day since we found out we were pregnant. This meant that instead of the thirty-second ultrasounds with brief check-up information, we would get to look at our little miracle for an hour while the technician did an in-depth scan of the baby. For the first time, we got to see definitive features of the baby, and our hearts melted. Everything from each vertebra of the spine, the hemispheres of the brain, chambers of the heart (beating at 146 bpm this go-around) and all the way to counting each finger and toe; our baby was in absolute perfect condition in every aspect, and we were over the moon. At one point, the baby curled its right hand in a ball and stuck its pointer finger directly at us. We are not sure if the baby was thinking, "Hey, that's my mom and dad" or "Hey, guys, don't forget I'm #1!" Regardless, it was right either way! When trying to get the perfect picture of the baby's profile for us to have as a keepsake, the baby kept turning its head and staring at us through the screen. The technology of this time and age was incredible to see each specific feature. However, there was one feature we turned our heads to the side for. To the appointment, we brought an envelope, and when it was time to peek at the gender of the baby, we opted to have the technician write the result on a piece of paper and keep it a secret. With there not being as many surprises in life as special as this one, we wanted to be surrounded by friends and family when finding out if Baby Marks was a boy or girl. A true test of patience was required of us for the next month until our party.

Butterfly kisses or baseball wishes was the theme of our gender reveal/baby shower that was held on August 29, 2020. Fifty of our closest family members and friends gathered at a park in Wisconsin to celebrate alongside of us. I decided that this strong momma-to-be needed some well-deserved pampering that morning, so I headed off to the salon to get my hair and makeup professionally done. By the time I left, I looked like a completely different person than when I arrived, and I was in love with the look they gave me. I wore a long white dress with colorful butterflies that decorated the fabric from top to bottom, and my husband wore his custom-made baseball jersey that I had given him two months prior for a Father's Day gift. The jersey read "Best Dad 20" on the back. Together we fit the theme of our big day perfectly.

When we pulled up to the park, the pavilion was completely decked out in decorations full of balloons, signs, our baby pictures, gorgeous table coverings with centerpieces, and streamers blowing in the wind—a lot of wind. Despite some intense winds that day, it was sunny and in the midseventies. If you know anything about Wisconsin and the unpredictable weather we get, you know that this weather was an incredible blessing in order for us to celebrate. Everyone started to show up; pictures were taken by our professional photographer to capture all the great moments and people in our lives, and the time had finally arrived after all the waiting and wondering. It was time to reveal if Baby Marks was a boy or a girl. We stood under streamers where a black balloon drop bag hung above our heads that our two very close friends prepared for us as they kept the secret for over a month to create this once in a lifetime surprise. After a group countdown from five, Chris pulled the string and out flew a ton of pink balloons. Baby Marks is a girl! The crowd cheered and cried, as did we.

It was the most surreal and perfect moment we could have ever asked for!

After our hearts stopped racing, and the high of the excitement died down a bit, it was time to enjoy some delicious food that was catered in from a local sub shop. We sat and mingled with our guests and tried to enjoy every moment. The day was going by so fast at this point. Before opening our ginormous amount of gracious gifts that everyone brought with them, we had a surprise of our own for everyone. We stood up in front of the crowd and called up my brother, Brandon, and his then fiancé, now wife, Kegan, to join us front and center. With them standing by our side, I read them a letter we wrote full of appreciation for all they have done to support us emotionally throughout every step of our journey. We handed them cards with scratch-off hearts on them. Very anxiously and with many emotions flying, they scratched the heart that revealed the big surprise. We asked them to be our baby's godparents, and they said yes. There were not many dry eyes at the park after this occurred. That moment was everything we had hoped it would be. We wrapped up our day of celebration by opening gifts and indulging in the incredibly decorated cookies and cupcakes that filled the dessert table. All this took place in a matter of four hours. When we got home that afternoon, with our baby girl's room now full of so many items we could no longer see carpet, we crashed on the couch and looked at each other. We could not believe the day was over already. If we thought our wedding day went fast four years prior, this day went faster than the speed of light. Our faces hurt from smiling so much, and that is how we knew it was the most perfect day either of us could have ever imagined. We worked so hard to be able to have this party of our own after celebrating so many other friends and babies over the years. We felt grateful beyond words. Of all the titles Chris and I have held, we knew that being classified as a "girl mom" and "girl dad" was going to be our favorite titles yet.

If we fast-forward to October, that put us well into the third trimester. They say it goes by fast, and sure at times it did, but for me personally, the time dragged on. It could be because I was just as sick as I was at the beginning of the pregnancy and wanted to crawl out of my own skin. I give endless amounts of credit to any woman who decides to put her body through pregnancy more than once. Overall, I would consider myself a very strong and resilient person, but this whole pregnancy situation had me complaining so many times throughout the day that I lost track. From the sleepless nights, abdominal discomfort from limbs jabbing me in places I did not know existed, back pain that felt like I had an elephant inside of me and not a four-pound tiny human, and all the other side effects; it was becoming harder as each day passed to look on the bright side of things. Everyone says that she will be worth it, and they are not wrong. She is absolutely one million times worth it all, but it does not discount the fact that my body feels like it has been through the ringer these days. I have completed the entire nesting phase—this has included having every cabinet and drawer in our home completely decluttered and organized, getting her room ready for her arrival, having car seats installed, and our bags packed and ready to go. Now I just needed to push through these final weeks, and she would be in our arms filling our lives with more sleepless nights soon enough, and it will be worth every single step of this crazy rollercoaster of a journey.

Speaking of a crazy rollercoaster, with all that we have been through, our story would never be complete without a little scare to round off this pregnancy experience. I was experiencing stomach pains on the date that marked my thirty-third week. When I explained my symptoms to my doctor's office, they suspected it was highly possible that I picked up a gallbladder infection. I went in to be seen, and after an examination, she changed her mind and was not leaning that way anymore but rather wanted to hook me up to a nonstress test to see what could be going on. After forty minutes, she looked at the report and determined I was having contractions as close as two minutes apart. She sent me to the main hospital at that point for almost six hours of observation. The contractions never stopped, and the doctors determined that they would not be stopping at that point but rather their goal would be for them to taper off and space out further. My cervix was completely closed, and there was zero concern that she would be coming right away on her own. They gave me the option of staying in the hospital for more monitoring, or I could just go home and self-monitor the situation while looking out for a handful of red flags. I opted to head home.

The suggestions they gave me for the next few weeks were to relax as much as possible, watch movies, drink water, take baths, and use Tylenol if needed. If the hardest part of all that was getting my sweatpants on, it did not sound like the worst-case scenario anymore. The two main red flags to look out for were if her movement slowed down throughout the day and if within a one-hour time span I had contractions consistently every three to five minutes. Luckily, for the most part she is extremely active, leaving zero concern in that department. But when you spend days in a row having contractions so often it feels like you do not remember a time not feeling the pain, it becomes exhausting and frustrating on a whole new level. My patience level has dropped below negative and even the littlest of nothings make me feel annoyed. It is like an out-of-body experience I wish was not a part of my story because no one wishes to feel this way. The only way I can describe it is that your body no longer feels like you once remember it. You become uncomfortable at all hours of the day that sometimes just being mad releases some of the physical and emotional pain so that for one second, you can feel the release of all the frustrations. Unfortunately, it is not fair to those around you because none of it is their fault, but you use them as an outlet—especially your spouse. So, for all the significant others out there who have a pregnant woman in their lives, please forgive us. We are not ourselves. We just want to feel normal again, and the days feel like years as we wait for the day our baby decides to really make her appearance and not just trick us with false trials.

That previous trip to the hospital unfortunately was not my only one prior to her arrival. I ended up back in labor and delivery two other times. Once was for what I thought were full-on labor contractions just to be sent home to be told it was false, and the other was for signs of dehydration and potential preeclampsia. Luckily, all tests cleared me of any issues, but it was scary, nonetheless. Some different medications were given to me to help curb my nausea, which was going at full throttle with no sign of letting up. At this point, I was dilated at 1 cm for a full month with zero hope of her coming just a little bit early to give me some relief. Needless to say, I was not only counting down the days at this point, but I was basically counting down the hours and minutes. I was ready for her whenever she was ready to make her official debut!

6

The One Worth Fighting For

Ready or not; here she comes! You plan, and God laughs! Whichever universal cliché you want to use to describe the day that our baby girl made her arrival, no words will ever do it justice. At 1:00 a.m. on December 9, 2020, our alarms buzzed, and we got ourselves together to head to the hospital for our 3:00 a.m. planned induction. We kissed our furry fifty-pound goldendoodle goodbye and told him that this time we would be returning with a new member of our family. We were full of so much joy and anticipation on the drive to the hospital. It was such a crazy concept to us that the next time we would be driving in our car there would be another human being in the backseat who we would be responsible for all the remaining days of our lives. We were assigned our room, and I changed into that ugly green oversized hospital gown that immediately makes you feel like a ginormous unattractive balloon. The doctor came in to check how far along I was, and to no surprise to me at all, I was still only 1 cm dilated. So, before any Pitocin could be administered, they had to try a different medication to attempt to speed things along. The first round did nothing for me, so they did a second round four hours later. Thankfully, the second round did what it was supposed to, so we were able to progress to Pitocin.

My birthing plan was to do everything naturally. Seeing as this would be my only birth ever, I wanted to feel it all so I knew first-hand what the hype was all about when women would say, "it is the worst pain you will ever feel." Well, I made it to level four of the Pitocin being administered, and I was twelve hours into the labor process when I hysterically cried into the eyes of my nurse and said, "Give me the epidural, now!" At this point the last check that was done showed that I was at 2.5 cm along, and I was never rechecked preepidural being administered by a very fast-talking Russian doctor who made me feel far from comforted. An hour and a half passed, and the nurse said she felt like it would be too early to check me, but she did it anyway. Just after 6:00 p.m., Chris was about to order his dinner to the room since the doctor guessed we would not be welcoming our baby into this world until the middle of the night sometime. To our surprise, the nurse looked at us and said, "Wow, you are at 10 cm already. Dad, grab a leg. It is time to push." We had zero time to process the words coming out of her mouth because I was completely numb from the pelvis down to my toes, and none of us expected this part of the process to arrive for at least another six hours.

For three straight hours with approximately one- to two-minute breaks, I pushed with every ounce of energy I could muster, but nothing I was doing was working. We reached the point where my next option was to push with the use of the vacuum device that attached to her head to give me 30 percent assistance. Nine pushes later, at 9:16 p.m., the most gorgeous eight-pound, 20.5-inch-long girl was placed on my chest. At that moment, everything else in the world disappeared. Jayda Mercy Marks came into our lives, and our hearts were immediately forever changed. I wish that this is where our birthing story could end and that it was all butterflies and rainbows after that moment, but unfortunately, we were faced with a much different situation.

Jayda was taken away from me to be checked out, and thankfully she was incredibly healthy from head to toe. On the contrary, I was not. My body began convulsing, and the doctors and nurses all said it was completely normal and within an hour it would go away. All but one nurse left the room as they chalked up the situation to it being a hormonal imbalance that they have seen many times before. After spending a few minutes holding Jayda and then needing to hand her over to Chris due to my uncontrollable shaking; the one nurse left in the room came over to check my stomach. She pressed on my stomach, and with big, wide eyes, I looked at her and said I felt like something just fell out of me. She lifted the sheet, and the next thing we know she went on her radio and exclaimed, "Emergency team room four!" In flew twelve doctors and nurses, and we had no idea what was going on. The head doctor told us that there was a lot of blood loss accompanied by many clots that I was passing. Meanwhile, it was well over an hour, and my shaking only got worse. None of the doctors were willing to give me any medication to calm it down except for one. She stepped in and advocated for me. They pumped me full of a ton of heavy drugs to calm my body down the best they could as all the doctors continued to work on me. The only thought going through my mind at this point was that

I was on the verge of death. The head anesthesiologist came into the room to try to find any functional vein on my body to insert another IV line. Even with the assistance of a special machine, no vein could be found until his fifth try. At this point I was deemed in tachycardia with a resting heart rate of 185 beats per minute, and I had officially lost just shy of 2,000 mL of blood. To give you some insight, doctors will consider it hemorrhaging with blood loss at 500 mL. So, I was bleeding out at around four times the concerned amount. In came a nurse holding a cooler full of O+ blood in preparation for blood transfusions. Thankfully, my brilliant doctors and nurses got everything under control, and the bleeding and shaking all calmed down roughly two hours later. None of our family knew that Jayda came into the world yet at this point due to the emergency health scare with which we were faced. When Chris got a moment to breathe, he made the phone calls. It was a lot for everyone to process, but once everyone knew that I was no longer facing what felt like life or death in the moment, we were able to all enjoy the arrival of our extremely healthy baby girl.

Based on where my levels were at with the blood loss, I did end up needing two blood transfusions. The first one did not help me at all, but the second one the next day did exactly what it needed to. I began to feel better almost instantly after that second transfusion but spent an extra night in the hospital to continue to be monitored. Chris was instantly thrown into parenthood with little to no assistance from me and did a sensational job. To see our baby girl in his arms knowing she was as safe as she would ever be, made my heart happier than I could ever describe. As frantic as I was over those two days, my team at the hospital never seemed to fret; and if they did, they certainly never showed it. I would be lying if I said I did not think at some points I was going to die and leave my husband to be a single father to our newborn precious miracle. It was the scariest time in my life thus far, but in hindsight, I was in the best hands possible with a team of brilliant doctors and nurses who had everything under control from the moment they were paged into the room. We were discharged and sent home roughly sixty hours after we had arrived to begin the induction process. They were the wildest, most unpredictable sixty hours of our lives.

My journey is unique to me, but pieces might not be all that different from what some of you are currently facing or have faced in your past. My experiences came full circle from the moment that my heart hurt for those facing an infertility battle and deciding to donate my eggs to my own struggles that I later faced down the road. I am just an average girl living in Wisconsin with a story to tell in hopes that something that I said in my book can help at least one person in need to not feel alone. My biggest prayer is that everyone facing an invisible illness of any kind can feel known, seen, and understood. Know you are not alone; unfortunately, most people in your life probably will not get your pain, but there are some people who will give you the emotional support that you need. Lean on those people. The others might not mean to harm you; they just are not equipped to handle that level of empathy. It would be like if you walked up to a homeless person on the street and asked them to hand you a million dollars. They would not be able to do that because they can only give what they have. The same goes for empathy. Those who do not possess it cannot hand it out. Fight faithfully and know that I recognize the strength it takes to keep fighting when no one can see your pain.

PS, Jayda Mercy Marks, I did not forget about you. Earlier in this book I wrote acknowledgments as well as small letters to each of your siblings that went to Heaven far too soon in 2019. Mommy has words for you as well, my love. You are my "why." You are the reason I never gave up and kept fighting through every step in my journey. I told myself that I would see treatment all the way through until the end no matter what. If I would have given up, you would not be here with us today. However, little girl, I was not the only one who kept fighting. You are a warrior yourself. Only one embryo out of the original nineteen extracted survived. You, baby girl, are the survivor. You are my forever miracle. When I hold you in my arms and look into your eyes, everything else in the world disappears. I will always be your number one fan, and I pray that we have a relationship one day as strong as the one I was blessed to have with my mom—your grandma. It is a bond that can never be broken. A bond full of trust, forgiveness, and unconditional love always. I hope one day when you are old enough to read this book that you are as proud of me as I am of you. You are my last but certainly not least dedication, and I owe you more than you realize. I am indebted to God for life that He chose me to be your mom. Jayda Mercy Marks, you are the one worth fighting for.

Printed in the United States
by Baker & Taylor Publisher Services